primer, noun | ˈpri-mer |

1. *a textbook or introduction to a subject*
2. *a material used to prepare a surface for further treatment*
3. *a device or compound used to ignite an explosive charge*

This is the start of a conversation.

We want to talk theology and we want you to talk about it too. The whole idea of Primer is that it prepares you for that conversation.

Each issue takes one big area of doctrine and lays a foundation. We look at how people are talking about the doctrine today, and what good resources are out there. We dig out some treasures from church history to help us wrap our heads around the big ideas. We focus on what difference the truth makes to the way we live life and serve the church.

The conversation begins on these pages. We've left lots of room for you to make notes, to underline and highlight things. We've chosen the paper and the feel of the whole thing to encourage you to take this slowly. We could have put all this online and you might have downloaded it – you might even have skim read it – but we want to go a bit deeper. So make a date in the diary, turn off your devices, pull up a chair.

And then carry on the conversation. Primer *is something that you can* discuss with others. *Chew it over together. Study it with your elders or church leadership team, your ministers' fraternal or homegroup leaders. Invite a group of potential leaders in your church to get together and read an article at a time.*

There's more of an introduction to the ethos of Primer in the epilogue at the end of this issue, but for now just start at the first article and work your way through. In the first couple of articles I explain why we've chosen our first theme and lay out the big issues. After that, Fred Zaspel, John Stevens and several others join in the conversation. I hope you will too.

Find additional resources for this issue of *Primer* at **PrimerHQ.com**

Connect with us:

🐦 *@PrimerHQ*
f */PrimerHQ*

DAVID SHAW is the Editor of *Primer*. He is part-time Theological Adviser for FIEC and part-time lecturer in New Testament and Greek at Oak Hill Theological College, London. He's married to Jo and they have four children.

🐦 *@_david_shaw*

growing
gospel-driven
churches

fiec ⬡ the *FELLOWSHIP of INDEPENDENT*
EVANGELICAL CHURCHES

Primer is produced by the Fellowship of Independent Evangelical Churches (FIEC); a family of churches in Britain, working together to go and make disciples of Jesus Christ in every community. Find out more at *fiec.org.uk*

RALPH CUNNINGTON is married to Anna and dad to Sophie, Zach and Jacob. He is co–pastor of City Church Manchester, Research Associate at WEST, a member of the Theological Teams of FIEC and Affinity and editor of Affinity's theological journal *Foundations*.

 @RalphCunnington

DAVE PUTTICK is married to Meriel. He serves as Assistant Pastor at Emmanuel Church Canterbury, where he was previously an Intern. He is responsible for leading Emmanuel's student ministry.

JOHN STEVENS is FIEC's National Director, co-chairman of the *A Passion for Life* steering group, sits on the Steering Committee for New Word Alive, and is one of the elders of Christchurch Market Harborough. John is married to Ursula and they have four children.

 @_JohnStevens

BENJAMIN BRECKINRIDGE WARFIELD (1851–1921) was married to Annie and served as Professor of Theology at Princeton Seminary from 1887 to 1921. He was the author of several works, including *The Inspiration and Authority of the Bible*.

FRED ZASPEL is pastor at the Reformed Baptist Church of Franconia, and Professor of Systematic Theology at Calvary Baptist Seminary in Lansdale, Pennsylvania. He is the author of *The Theology of B.B. Warfield: A Systematic Summary* and *Warfield on the Christian Life: Living in Light of the Gospel*.

"We look to Thee to give us the fellowship of that Spirit who guided the prophets and apostles, that we may take their words in the sense in which they spoke and assign its right shade of meaning to every utterance."

Hilary of Poitiers' De Trinitate
(c. AD 350)

The Inspiration of Saint Matthew (1602) by Caravaggio

Defend a lion?

Agreeing and disagreeing with Spurgeon.

> *The best way to spread the Gospel is to spread the Gospel. I believe the best way of defending the Gospel is to spread the Gospel! I was addressing a number of students, the other day, upon the apologies for the Gospel which are so numerous just now. A great many learned men are defending the Gospel—no doubt it is a very proper and right thing to do—yet I always notice that when there are most books of that kind, it is because the Gospel, itself, is not being preached.*

CHARLES SPURGEON

> *Suppose a number of persons were to take it into their heads that they had to defend a lion, a full-grown king of beasts! There he is in a cage and here come all the soldiers of the army to fight for him. Well, I would suggest to them, if they would not object and feel that it was humbling to them, that they should kindly stand back, open the door, and let the lion out! I believe that would be the best way of defending him, for he would take care of himself—and the best "apology" for the Gospel is to let the Gospel out! Never mind about defending Deuteronomy or the whole of the Pentateuch— preach Jesus Christ and Him crucified! Let the Lion out and see who will dare to approach Him! The Lion of the tribe of Judah will soon drive away all His adversaries! This was how Christ's first disciples worked—they preached Jesus Christ wherever they went! They did not stop to apologise, but boldly bore their witness concerning Him.*

From the sermon entitled *'Christ and his Co-workers,'* preached June 10th 1886. See also *'The Lover of God's Law Filled With Peace,'* preached Jan 22nd 1882, and his address to the Annual Meeting of the British and Foreign Bible Society on May 5th 1875. Reassuringly, even the Prince of Preachers milked a good illustration when he had one!

The subject of this issue of Primer is *Scripture*. And yes, we're going to think about how to defend it.

Since we're about to ignore Spurgeon's advice we should at least recognise its value. Three things concern him: the danger of distraction from our main task of proclaiming the gospel; the arrogance of thinking that God's word needs our defence; and the risk of making Scripture only as reliable as our arguments: *"These props come down and then our adversaries think that the Book is down, too."* It's hard to disagree with any of those, but of course to say something can be done arrogantly or to the neglect of other things doesn't mean it can't be done well or shouldn't be done at all. Even Spurgeon thinks that: he says – defending the Bible is *"a very proper and right thing to do."* It is also, we would add, an important thing to do considering the context of pastoral ministry right now. Here are four reasons why:

First, it is a **perennial** issue. For as long as God has spoken to humanity, the authority and truthfulness of his word has been under attack: *"Did God really say?" "You will not certainly die"* (Gen 3:1, 4). A constant failing of God's people ever since has been to distrust God's word and reject his prophets. Correspondingly, the constant need of God's people is to know that God's word is utterly reliable and sufficient, that is, to know certain things about God's word and to have strong convictions about it under testing. That, after all, is what Jesus models when he is tempted: holding on to God's word where Adam fell, insisting *"it is written," "it is said"* (Luke 4:4, 8,

From the sermon
'The Lover of God's
Law Filled With
Peace.'

As we shall see, the challenge before us is not only that 'traditions of men' are set against the Bible in various ways, but also that people believe the Bible has a fundamentally human origin. That is, they see the Bible as a record of human encounters with God, essentially as a collection of human traditions that we must sift through for ourselves.

12). He defends himself with the conviction that God's word stands.

So the temptation to reject God's word is a perennial issue, but so too is the danger of confusing false prophecy or false teaching with God's word. Through the Old Testament God's people are warned about those who claim to speak for God but do not (Jer 23:16-22, Ezekiel 13), and likewise in the New Testament there are those who set the traditions of men over Scripture or peddle myths, turning away from the truth (Mark 7:1-13, Acts 20:29-30, 2 Tim 4:3-5, 2 Pet 3:16-2:3). And what did Jesus do when he met such ideas? He *defended* Scripture, refusing to allow people to *"nullify the Word of God"* (Mark 7:13).

Second, if someone has confidence in God's word it will help them to deal with every other issue they could face. In that sense it is a **foundational** issue. It's another lesson from Jesus. Whatever the theological challenge he often comes back to four simple words: *"have you not read?"* Thus the value of reflecting on the doctrine of Scripture is that it lays the foundation to address every other issue. This is especially important because many of the people we meet inside and outside our churches don't, deep down, think that what God has said settles the matter. All too often our criterion for what is true comes down to 'does it feel right?' 'Does it increase human happiness?' Our view of what is false is increasingly shaped by what we think will give offence or will negatively affect how people see themselves. So, spending some time on the foundational nature of Scripture is important, and part of that task will be addressing people's doubts, misunderstandings and misgivings about the reliability and truthfulness of Scripture.

A third, related, reason to address the issue is that it is a *visible* issue. The media regularly encourages those doubts and misgivings about the truthfulness of Scripture. Annually, around Christmas and Easter, there are high profile stories of scholars whose 'shocking' research casts doubt on the reliability of the Bible manuscripts or the reality of the events it describes. Last year, on December 23rd no less, Newsweek magazine ran a cover story entitled *'The Bible: So Misunderstood it's a Sin.'* In 2014 the BBC screened a two-part documentary about the 19th century discovery of Bible manuscripts that supposedly rocked the church, revealing we'd been reading the wrong Bible all this time. Or there's the drip feed of New Atheism, no better informed than a Dan Brown novel but casting aspersions like this:

> *To be fair, much of the Bible is not systematically evil but just plain weird, as you would expect of a chaotically cobbled-together anthology of disjointed documents, composed, revised, translated, distorted and 'improved' by hundreds of anonymous authors, editors and copyists, unknown to us and mostly unknown to each other, spanning nine centuries*

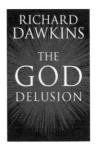

Richard Dawkins, *The God Delusion* (London: Random House, 2006), 278.

All of this means the people in our churches will have some level of awareness of these questions and will likely have some questions of their own. It means we meet these sorts of issues in our evangelistic groups. It is a *visible* issue.

Fourth, it is a *pressure* issue. It is getting harder to defend the Bible. Not because there are any better arguments about its reliability, but because our culture has taken several further steps away from its Christianised roots. The Bible's teachings on sexual ethics, the nature of marriage, and the authority structures within the family and the church, were once assumed, then quietly taken leave of, and now are deemed offensive or even dangerous. In that sense it's harder to defend the Bible.

There is also the kind of pressure the author Rob Bell captured in a recent appearance of the Oprah Winfrey show. When asked about the church's stance on homosexual marriage he said,

ROB BELL

I think culture is already there and the church will continue to be even more irrelevant when it quotes letters from 2,000 years ago as their best defence, when you have in front of you flesh-and-blood people who are your brothers and sisters, and aunts and uncles, and co-workers and neighbours, and they love each other and just want to go through life.

Peter Enns, *The Bible Tells Me So: Why Defending Scripture Has Made Us Unable to Read It* (San Francisco: HarperOne, 2014), 8.

Put simply, we are now surrounded by people we care about for whom the Bible is deeply offensive. It is a pressure issue because we have to look brothers and sisters and aunts and uncles and co-workers and neighbours in the eye knowing that to defend the Bible is to deny their lifestyles.

An important part of our task, therefore, is acknowledging this pressure and making space for people to wrestle with it, not least because there are wolves who will exploit it. Faced with the cultural shift but not wanting to abandon the Bible completely, there are now a number of prominent leaders who talk about the "Bible-induced stress" that comes from trying to defend it or from not being allowed to raise questions. Instead of committing to defend the Bible they are promoting a new and supposedly more faithful way of reading it. They still talk about championing the Bible. They still talk about loving Jesus, they still talk about his death on the cross. They want us to read the Bible and find Jesus at the heart of it, but they have found ways of reading it which means we don't need to defend the bits that our society finds offensive.

You can see how attractive that's going to be. You can also imagine how much air-time they will be able to get: "Prominent Christian leader says we've been reading the Bible wrong all these years." Even if people don't find it attractive, it can be very unsettling to hear ex-evangelicals saying, "when I was younger I used to read the Bible like that, I used to talk about inerrancy, but now I've read the Bible more closely and lived a little more I realise it's all a bit more complicated than that. We can't impose our frameworks on scripture. We just need to let the Bible be the Bible."

All of which means this is a **pastoral** issue. Of course Spurgeon is right, there's a sense in which we don't need to defend the lion, just let the Bible roar in our preaching. On the other hand it might help to think a bit differently about it. We don't need to defend the lion, but we do need to defend the sheep. To protect and nourish them. That will mean helping them to know how to answer some of these issues. To have confidence in God's word. To ask all who come: *"Have you not read?"*

To that end, this issue of Primer includes a tour of the contemporary challenges to the Bible and gives some ideas of how to respond and what's worth reading.

In all these debates the word 'inerrancy' has been celebrated, redefined or rejected in countless ways, and so John Stevens gives us a reflection on its current use, based on the recent *Five Views on Biblical Inerrancy* (Grand Rapids: Zondervan, 2013).

Next we want to help you make some old friends in Primer, and so we have an excerpt from B.B. Warfield's article on Inspiration. To guide our reading of that we have some help from Fred Zaspel, author of *The Theology of B. B. Warfield: A Systematic Summary* and *Warfield on the Christian Life*, who has introduced and annotated the text. As we'll see, Warfield plays the hero or the villain in many accounts of the doctrine of Scripture and so we wanted to go to the horse's mouth. The excerpt we have chosen describes the role human authors played in the writing of Scripture; an area which can help us to defend Scripture and also marvel at it.

The last three articles have a more practical focus: The first is an excerpt from a new book *Confident: Why We Can Trust the Bible* in which Dan Strange argues the Bible is *"reassuringly unfashionable."* It's a striking idea that should give us some confidence and proves to be a helpful evangelistic thought. Next we turn to the question of Old Testament violence, which is regularly cited as an argument against the Bible's authority. With that in mind Dave Puttick helps us think through one of the sharpest examples: the destruction of the Canaanites. The final piece before a closing epilogue is an interview with Ralph Cunnington, hearing how a recent church plant has been trying to develop a confidence in God's word at the start of their life together. In it Ralph shares some great encouragements and ideas about how to take these truths to defend, sustain and nourish the sheep. P

Mapping the Debate

The doctrine of Scripture in our contemporary context.

"Have you not read?" was one of Jesus' best questions. Four words which highlight the value Jesus placed on Scripture and the failure of the scribes, chief priests, elders, Pharisees and Sadducees to pay close enough attention.

It is an interesting twist, then, that a number of people who want to question a traditional understanding of Scripture are also quoting Jesus. "Have you not read?" they ask. "Because if you do read the Bible closely enough you realise that it is more complicated than you realise. It won't fit your neat systems. If you read carefully you realise that there is a mismatch between your *doctrine of Scripture* and the Scriptures themselves."

See e.g. *Inspiration and Incarnation: Evangelicals and the Problem of the Old Testament* (Grand Rapids: Baker Academic, 2005) and *The Bible Tells Me So: Why Defending Scripture Has Made Us Unable to Read It* (San Francisco: HarperOne, 2014) both by Peter Enns; Kenton L. Sparks, *God's Word in Human Words: An Evangelical Appropriation of Critical Biblical Scholarship* (Grand Rapids: Baker, 2008); Christian Smith, *The Bible Made Impossible: Why Biblicism is not a Truly Evangelical Reading of Scripture* (Grand Rapids: Brazos Press, 2012).

A whole host of issues are contained within those questions and we will spend the rest of this issue of Primer teasing them out. In this article the goal is simply to map out the main areas of debate and give some pointers along the way to explore the issues more fully.

A helpful way in will be to focus on one of the central questions: *where does our doctrine of Scripture come from?* There are two aspects to this question:

First, have we formed our views about Scripture by reading Scripture or by imposing some sort of framework from outside?

Second, have we read carefully enough everything we find inside the Bible and allowed that to shape how we think about it?

In both cases there's an accusation of hypocrisy or at least inconsistency. If evangelicals are really people of the Bible why do they not read it more carefully and just let the Bible be the Bible?

Let's take these two aspects in turn.

1. Have frameworks been imposed on the Bible from outside?

There are various periods in church history where it is suggested that the doctrine of Scripture becomes hijacked by a theological or philosophical agenda. In some accounts, the villain of the piece is Anselm (the 12th century Archbishop of Canterbury) and his concept of God as "a being than which no greater can be conceived." Anselm developed this thought into a proof for the existence of God (the ontological argument) but the key issue is the assumption that God is the greatest of all possible beings; in other words, perfect. From there it might be (and has been) argued that since God is perfect, his word must be perfect and without any mistakes of any kind. So, you can see how the accusation arises: we have begun with a logical premise – God is a perfect being – and imposed that concept, and our definition of perfection, onto the Bible.

A second villain in some people's minds is Francis Turretin in the seventeenth century. An influential book by Rogers and McKim, for example, argued that he represents a high point of Reformed Scholasticism (which surely sounds like a bad thing to be) and "radically departed from the approach of Calvin by resting belief in the authority of Scripture on rational proofs of its inspiration and inerrancy."

The third and most popular villain, however, is B.B. Warfield, along with his Princeton colleague A.A. Hodge. Both were writing and teaching at a time when the historical accuracy of the Bible was coming under unprecedented scrutiny with the development of historical criticism. In the attempt to defend the Bible they wrote a number of highly influential works. For our purposes we need to know that they too stand accused of imposing a rationalistic concept of "inerrancy" on the Bible. And, because they were writing relatively recently, inerrancy gets criticised for being a *modern* as well as a *foreign* imposition on the Bible.

It is worth noticing that there is a form of this argument that is enormously helpful. After all, the Bible reveals God to be perfect in all his ways and specifically, to be perfectly true and consistent in all he says and does (Numbers 23:19, Isaiah 45:19, Psalm 33:4). So there is a biblical argument from God's perfections to be made and ultimately we do trust the Bible because God does not lie and is true to his word. See e.g. Paul Helm, "The Perfect Trustworthiness of God," in *The Trustworthiness of God: Perspectives on the Nature of Scripture* (Leicester: Apollos, 2002), 237–52.

Jack B. Rogers and Donald K. McKim, *The Authority and Interpretation of the Bible: An Historical Approach* (New York: Harper & Row, 1979), 176. For a helpful response and discussion of Turretin as he relates to Calvin's views on Scripture, see Ralph Cunnington, "Did Turretin Depart from Calvin's View on the Concept of Error in the Scriptures?," *Foundations* 61 (2011): 41–58.

See chiefly B.B. Warfield and A. Hodge, "Inspiration," *The Presbyterian Review* 6 (1881): 225–60; Warfield, The Inspiration and Authority of the Bible (London: Marshall, Morgan & Scott, 1951). The significance of Warfield and Hodge as 'Old Princetonians' taking their stand against modernism is hard to overestimate and interest in their legacy endures. See e.g. Fred G. Zaspel, *The Theology of B. B. Warfield: A Systematic Summary* (Wheaton, Ill.: Crossway, 2010).

1.1 Is inerrancy a foreign concept imposed on the Bible?

One helpful way to answer the question might be to see how Warfield and Hodge describe the way the church developed its view of Scripture's truthfulness and inerrancy:

> *The primary ground on which it has been held by the Church as the true doctrine is that it is the doctrine of Biblical writers themselves, and has therefore the whole mass of evidence for it which goes to show that the Biblical writers are trustworthy as doctrinal guides.*

The Inspiration and Authority of the Bible (London: Marshall, Morgan and Scott, 1951), 173.

"Now if this doctrine is to be assailed on critical grounds, it is very clear that, first of all, criticism must be required to proceed against the evidence on which it is based. This evidence, it is obvious, is twofold. First, there is the exegetical evidence that the doctrine held and taught by the Church is the doctrine held and taught by the Biblical writers themselves. And secondly, there is the whole mass of evidence—internal and external, objective and subjective, historical and philosophical, human and divine—which goes to show that the Biblical writers are trustworthy as doctrinal guides. If they are trustworthy teachers of doctrine and if they held and taught this doctrine, then this doctrine is true, and is to be accepted and acted upon as true by us all." Ibid., 174.

Put simply we get our doctrine of Scripture from what Scripture says about itself. Recognising that others are rejecting inerrancy, Warfield and Hodge go on to set them their task: They either have to prove that the biblical writers did not hold to a view of inerrancy or that we cannot trust them even though they did. Strikingly then, Warfield is not arguing his case by adopting modernist or rationalistic presuppositions. Rather, he is trying to force the argument back to exegesis asking: *"What does the Bible say about itself?"* From there, Warfield builds his case, always aware of the human authors' involvement in the process of inspiration, but never allowing that to detract from the Bible's utter trustworthiness.

The whole argument of *Inspiration and Authority* ch3 examines the exegetical evidence. In this way, Warfield paves the way for later works like John Wenham's *Christ and the Bible* (London: Tyndale, 1970).

1.2 Is inerrancy a new idea?

Ernest Sandeen, *The Origins of Fundamentalism: Toward A Historical Interpretation* (Philadelphia: Fortress, 1968), 14.

Well yes. And no. When the claim is made that *"the doctrine of inerrancy in the original autographs did not exist in either Europe or America prior to its formulation in the last half of the nineteenth century"* we need to distinguish a few things. It is certainly true that the term "inerrancy" began to be applied to Scripture in the late nineteenth century. On the other hand of course a concept can exist before technical terms are coined to describe it. For example, the first reference in written works to "church planting" that I can find occurs in 1961, but I take it churches were planted and the activity of church planting was recognised prior to that. So too with the inerrancy of Scripture. That English term is not used prior to the nineteenth century but Calvin speaks of Scripture being "without error", and before him Augustine spoke to reverencing the Scriptures above every other text for they alone are *"free from error."*

Woodbridge catalogues the historical evidence in *Biblical Authority: A Critique of the Rogers/McKim Proposal*, (Grand Rapids: Zondervan, 1982). For a briefer and more up to date overview see his "Evangelical Self-Identity and the Doctrine of Biblical Inerrancy," in *Understanding the Times: New Testament Studies in the 21st Century: Essays in Honor of D. A. Carson on the Occasion of His 65th Birthday* (Wheaton: Crossway, 2011), 104–38.

Next we should notice that the claim is a little more specific, namely that the doctrine of inerrancy *in the original autographs* did not exist until this period (autographs meaning the manuscripts originally written by the hand of the authors or their amanuenses [those who wrote down what the authors dictated, e.g. Tertius in Rom 16:22]).

But even this is not a novel idea, as is clear, for example, in a famous passage in Augustine's letters where he describes his thought process when he meets an apparent contradiction in Scripture:

> *I have learned to yield this respect and honour only to the canonical books of Scripture: of these alone do I most firmly believe that the authors were completely free from error. And if in these writings I am perplexed by anything which appears to me opposed to truth, I do not hesitate to suppose that either the manuscript is faulty, or the translator has not caught the meaning of what was said, or I myself have failed to understand it.*

Letter 82, Augustine to Jerome.

So for Augustine the authors were completely free from error but there is the possibility that the manuscripts which transmit their text are faulty. In other words, Augustine clearly believes that inerrancy belongs to the texts as originally given - the same point Warfield is making by speaking about the autographs. So no, this is not a new idea.

Going Deeper: *Thinking about Autographs*

This language of the "inerrancy of the original autographs" is much disputed. For some, it is a useless claim because we do not possess those original manuscripts. For others, it is a sign that we have tied ourselves in knots and do not need to imagine flawless manuscripts and instead just embrace the messiness of Scripture. In Warfield's work it is actually a sign that he was alert to the dangers of claiming too much. He does not claim that the transmission of manuscripts was inerrant. He knew that mistakes could and did creep in as manuscripts were copied and texts were translated. For that reason he spoke of the inerrancy of the original autographs – i.e. arguing that God's supervision ensured that perfectly true revelation was made to and through human authors and recorded perfectly.

Nevertheless, we need to be a little careful about how we express the idea of autographs. Some books of the Bible clearly had editors who arranged material by other authors and we would want to say that God inspired that process as much as he inspired the authors. The final form of the books are inerrant as well as the original textual sources for books such as Deuteronomy and Psalms.

On the other hand we do not need to be too troubled that we do not have the autographs themselves because, as Michael Kruger has been arguing recently, the manuscripts we do have enable us to establish the vast majority of the original text. In that sense, we do have the autographical text – it is preserved in the manuscripts that have come down to us.

Hence the way that the UCCF and FIEC Doctrinal Bases speak of the inspiration of the Bible "as originally given" being without error.

See e.g. michaeljkruger.com/some-optimism-in-textual-criticism/

Nor is Warfield necessarily making a theological mountain out of an exegetical molehill by placing such emphasis on this point. In fact, what is happening is the same thing that has happened throughout church history. When a doctrine comes under attack the church is forced (and blessed) to define more carefully how it understands what it previously might have taken for granted. It happened with Christology in the councils and creeds of the fourth and fifth centuries; it has been happening with the relationship between justification and good works since the sixteenth century; and it has been happening with Scripture since the serious challenges to the reliability of the Bible arose in the nineteenth century. Until that point, the inerrancy of the Bible had been largely assumed, now it needed to be defined and defended more carefully.

In summary then, the accusation that all this talk of inerrancy represents an imposition onto Scripture of a late and rationalistic framework is unfounded. Now we turn to the various features of the Bible that some people argue mean we still need to rethink our doctrine of Scripture.

2. Are there features inside the Bible that demand a rethink?

Here we are going to consider two things: the humanity of scripture, and the diversity of scripture.

2.1 The humanity of Scripture

God spoke through human authors. Those human authors were sinful human beings, they were limited in their knowledge and understanding, and they were products of their Ancient Near Eastern or first century Graeco-Roman worlds. On those facts everyone would agree. The question though is what impact those facts have on our doctrine of Scripture. What does this very basic feature of the Bible, its dual authorship, mean for the Bible?

Two conclusions are sometimes drawn. The first assumes the old saying "to err is human" is true and applies it to the Bible – if the humanity of the authors was left intact, their failings will show through. One classic example comes from C. S. Lewis' discussion of the psalms:

"

The human qualities of the raw materials show through. Naïvety, error, contradiction, even (as in the cursing Psalms) wickedness are not removed. The total result is not "the Word of God" in the sense that every passage, in itself, gives impeccable science or history. It carries the Word of God; and we (under grace, with attention to tradition and to interpreters wiser than ourselves, and with the use of such intelligence and learning as we may have) receive that word from it not by using it as an encyclopaedia or an encyclical but by steeping ourselves in its tone or temper and so learning its overall message.

It is certainly true though that 'inerrancy' has, in the North American context, sometimes been too narrowly defined and used to defend certain interpretations of Scripture rather than to describe one of its properties. For more reflection in inerrancy in the contemporary debate, see John Stevens' article on page 24.

C. S. Lewis, *Reflections on the Psalms* (London: Harper Collins, 1977), 94. Lewis goes on to say that this is something we just need to accept. We might have expected "an unrefracted light giving us ultimate truth in systematic form – something we could have tabulated and memorised and relied upon like a multiplication table" but he did not give us one and ultimately he knows best.

We will come back to thinking about what that means for how we read the Bible, for now we just note the argument he is making: the sinfulness and the limitations of the human authors remains in Scripture.

The second and more common argument is also a more subtle one. The result is often the same but it sounds less controversial. The argument is simply that God chose to work through human authors, who lived at certain times and in certain places and they wrote in the terms and language and with the presuppositions of their own time. This means that God spoke to people in terms they could understand, based on how they already understood the world, and they in turn spoke of God in the terms of their culture. This extends not only to how they describe the physical world or reflect their cultural expressions (think sandal-swapping to seal a deal in Ruth 4:7 or grabbing hold of someone's thigh when you make an oath, Gen 24:9) but also to the way they conceive of God himself.

Peter Enns, for example, thinks this is a helpful way to approach the idea that God fought for his people in the OT and commanded the destruction of the Canaanites:

*The Bible
Tells Me So,*
62–63.

The Bible – from front to back – is the story of God told from the limited point of view of real people living at a certain place and time. It is not like the Israelites were debating whether or not to go ahead and describe God as a mighty warrior. They had no choice. That's just how it was done – that was their cultural language. And if the writers had somehow been able to step outside of their culture and invent a new way of talking, their story would have made no sense to anyone else. The Bible looks this way because 'God lets his children tell the story,' so to speak.

So here the point is that human authors are culture bound. The result is that just like in C.S. Lewis' approach, we need to recognise that God's word does not reflect him perfectly, and so we need to see how the narrative of Scripture develops and to "steep ourselves in its tone or temper and so learn its overall message." That way we can filter out the culturally-conditioned distortions of who God is from the more abiding and eternal truths.

How then to respond to this argument?

1. First it is worth noting that Enns spends half of his book discussing the Canaanite destruction, and with good reason. He knows that people struggle with "God's seemingly over-the-top knee-jerk violence in the Old Testament, and especially Canaanite extermination, which some contemporary atheists hail as exhibit A for the utter stupidity of any faith in the God of the Bible."

*The Bible
Tells Me So,*
67.

See Dave Puttick's article on page 58 for more help with this.

And of course he is right. Not that anything in the Old Testament is "over-the-top," but he is right that many people do struggle with these issues and that the Joshua narrative is out there as Exhibit A. That means we ought to make sure that within our churches there is space for people to wrestle with these issues and that our expository teaching does spend time in Old Testament narratives so that we can debunk some of the myths about these passages and help people see how they fit in to salvation history and how they point to Christ.

2. We also ought not to lose sight of the truth that is being asserted here. God did speak to "real people living at a certain place and time" and we certainly do need to take account of that as we read the Bible. As Don Carson has helpfully argued, knowledge of the historical context of the Old and New Testaments is crucial to accurately translate, interpret and apply God's word. Nor should we see this historical locatedness as just a necessary evil. The fact that we get a developing sense of what it looks like to live faithfully in different circumstances and at different stages of salvation history means that we are helped to imagine what it will look like for us to do so in whatever place or time we find ourselves. In the same way Paul's letters are not abstract doctrinal summaries but "timely words to concrete situations which are prototypes of our own" modelling for us how to defend and grow in the gospel according to the needs of different people and contexts.

Search *thegospelcoalition.org* for 'mastered by the book.'

Leander Keck, quoted in J. Christiaan Beker, *Paul the Apostle: The Triumph of God in Life and Thought* (Edinburgh: T&T Clark, 1980).

3. On the other hand we need to recognise the truth that is missing here: namely the *dual* authorship of Scripture. Enns speaks of God's children telling the story, not of God telling his story through his children which is the clear way in which Scripture presents itself. Yes he speaks to them in ways they can understand, sensitive to their language and culture, but why should that mean that the result is simply human authors giving voice to the values of their cultures? And how could anyone read the Bible and think that description is apt? The human authors suffered terribly, precisely because they were out of step with their cultures and confronted them with God's word. Enns' model simply cannot account for the persecution of the prophets and the apostles, or for God's reassurance that the rejection of the prophets is actually a rejection of God himself (1 Sam 8:7; cf. Luke 10:16, 1 Thess 4:8).

E.g. the thought of prophets speaking "from God, carried along by the Holy Spirit" (2 Peter 1:21), or Paul's sense of being commissioned by God and speaking in Christ (2 Cor 2:17).

4. We also need to recognise that the appeal of this argument is precisely the way it allows us to keep reading the Bible without allowing it to confront us or feeling the need to defend it where it clashes with our secular culture.

5. A helpful response then might be to draw attention to the way in which Enns conceives of the modern day reader. His whole book is dedicated to those who think out loud and calls us to wrestle with the Bible and to find Jesus in it. In other words, we are able to think for ourselves. Apparently then not everyone is so culture bound that they can only repeat the presuppositions of their culture. Only people in the fourth century B.C. and first century A.D. Intriguing, and rather convenient.

6. We might also ask what this approach actually does to our knowledge of God. We are left with trying to sort out what C.S. Lewis calls the "overall message" from amongst the various culture-bound and mistaken ideas. Often what happens is that the culturally-conditioned material turns out to be what we, in a secular twenty-first Century Western context, find offensive, and the "overall message," in the case of someone like Steve Chalke turns out to be the vague notion that "God is love." But how do we know that? And on what grounds? If you say you think the parable of the prodigal son is the truest expression of who God is (open arms, unconditionally receiving people back without any need for atonement) and I think the parable of the tenants has it right (God throws out people who disrespect his Son) which one of us is right? Why?

2.2 The diversity of Scripture

Here our attention turns to whether traditional views of the Bible can stand up to the diversity we find within it. Steve Chalke thinks it cannot: The Bible

" *contains various, sometimes harmonious, sometimes discordant, sometimes even contradictory voices, each of which contributes to the developing story of humanity's moral and spiritual imagination, which through this conversation is challenged, stretched and constantly enlarged.*

Restoring Confidence in the Bible, available online: *oasisuk.org/theology-resources*. Notice again the exclusive emphasis on human authorship.

Two elements there mean Steve Chalke thinks those contradictory voices are a good thing. First, the idea that humanity's moral and spiritual imagination is an evolving, developing thing and so some change and disagreement with the past is a good thing. We will come back to that thought in a minute. Then there is the thought that Scripture is essentially a constantly enlarged "conversation." I suspect this is the main appeal of this approach. If we can say that there is debate and disagreement within the Bible and God is okay with that then we have to say there should be debate and disagreement in the church and God is okay with that too. It means people can disagree about the nature of the atonement, the truthfulness of the Bible, the morality of same sex relationships and the only mistake would be to stifle the "conversation." That is what God would be against.

Alternatively, diversity is sometimes used to argue that the Bible simply isn't clear. There are conflicting ideas and so it means we have to suspend judgment. Indeed sometimes it is claimed that because interpreters disagree about a passage it means we really cannot be certain what it means. George Guthrie highlights an example of this in a recent book arguing for the acceptability of homosexual relationships. Although the author promises to examine the biblical texts he does not actually make many interpretative decisions. Instead, in Guthrie's words, he "simply trots out a variety of opinions that provide alternatives to the historic Christian view, leading us enthusiastically to the scrolls of ancient Scripture only to leave them tied up on the desk, often choked with the variegated cords of scholarly opinion."

See his review of David Gushee's *Changing Our Mind* (Canton, MI: David Crumm Media, LLC, 2014) online here: *thegospelcoalition.org/article/changing-our-mind*

Of course, some passages of Scripture are hard to interpret, but we need to beware arguments that throw their hands up and say no-one really knows what these passages mean, especially when they are ignoring the plain teaching of Scripture that, for example, monogamous heterosexual relationships are the biblical model.

We will think about how to respond to the diversity of the Bible, but first it will help to establish what diversity and 'contradiction' is being highlighted. If we fold in the contributions of Bart Ehrman, Steve Chalke, and Peter Enns, we can categorise them as follows:

Going deeper: *The analogy of the incarnation*

An idea you often read in relation to the human authorship of Scripture is that a comparison with the doctrine of the incarnation might be helpful.

The argument goes something like this: Jesus has a divine and a human nature. The Bible has a divine and human author and so we can think about them in similar ways. Enthusiasm for how fruitful this comparison might be varies rather a lot, and as Don Carson points out, the crucial thing is to identify the point of the comparison carefully rather than waving around terms like incarnation: "whenever one makes an entire argument turn on analogy, it is imperative to explain in what ways the two poles of the analogy are alike and unlike."

D. A. Carson, Collected Writings on Scripture (IVP, 2010), 269.

In this case, with Christ we are talking about two natures, divine and human, combined in one person, the man Jesus Christ. With Scripture we are talking about two persons, God and the human author, combining to produce a text. Furthermore, Christ, as God the Son

incarnate, is divine and therefore a proper object of our worship. The Bible is not itself divine, or an object of worship, but is a divine act of communication of our God, and he is to be worshipped.

So it is not a close analogy and the uniqueness of the incarnation in those respects means Tim Ward believes that "this kind of analogy between Scripture and incarnation is of very limited value." Duly warned, I think we can still draw three helpful comparisons. The first can be found in Herman Bavinck's Reformed Dogmatics:

Words of Life: Scripture as the Living and Active Word of God (Nottingham: IVP, 2009), 77.

"Christ became flesh, a servant, without form or comeliness, the most despised of human beings; he descended to the nethermost parts of the earth and became obedient even to death on the cross. So also the word, the revelation of God, entered the world of creatureliness, the life and history of humanity, in all the human forms of dream and vision, of investigation and reflection, right down into that which is humanly weak and despised and ignoble."

Herman Bavinck, *Reformed Dogmatics, Vol. 1: Prolegomena*, ed. John Bolt (Grand Rapids: Baker Academic, 2003), 434.

Contradictions within a single book or author: Bart Ehrman, for example, thinks he has found one in John's Gospel:

One of my favourite apparent discrepancies—I read John for years without realizing how strange this one is—comes in Jesus' 'Farewell Discourse,' the last address that Jesus delivers to his disciples, at his last meal with them, which takes up all of chapters 13 to 17 in the Gospel according to John. In John 13:36, Peter says to Jesus, 'Lord, where are you going?' A few verses later, Thomas says, 'Lord, we do not know where you are going' (John 14:5). And then, a few minutes later, at the same meal, Jesus upbraids his disciples, saying, 'Now I am going to the one who sent me, yet none of you asks me, "Where are you going?"' (John 16:5). Either Jesus had a very short attention span or there is something strange going on with the sources for these chapters, creating an odd kind of disconnect.

Bart D. Ehrman, *Jesus, Interrupted: Revealing the Hidden Contradictions in the Bible (And Why We Do not Know About Them)* (Harper Collins, 2009), 9.

In other words, Bavinck sees a consistent divine modus operandi at work in both the incarnation and the inspiration of the Bible. In Paul Wells' words: "It is part of the scandal of the gospel. God's Son appeared as a servant and his word assumed a self-effacing and modest exterior." Or, as C.S. Lewis rightly points out, if we can get our heads around the Son being nursed at the breast of a peasant girl, we should not be surprised if he is preached in the common language of his day or if his teachings are recorded in that same language.

Taking the Bible at Its Word (Ross-shire: Christian Focus, 2013), 160.

See his "Introduction" to J. B. Phillips, *Letters to Young Churches: A Translation of the New Testament Epistles* (New York: Macmillan, 1953), vii-viii.

Second, we can go a little further with Paul Wells who suggests that "the advantage of the Christological parallel is that illustrates how real humanity is possible without implying sin, fallibility or error." Put simply, if you're saying that a genuinely human element must involve sin then how can you have a sinless Jesus? If he could have a human nature and yet be without sin, why cannot God use a human author to produce a sinless, errorless Bible?

Taking the Bible at Its Word, 158.

Lastly, the incarnation reminds us that you can fall off a horse on both sides. When we talk about Jesus we need to uphold his full humanity (without which he cannot represent us) and his full divinity (without which he cannot reveal God to us or save us). We cannot say he only appeared to be a human (the heresy of docetism) and we cannot say he was somehow less than God (the heresies of Arianism/adoptionism). The reason this is important is that evangelicals are occasionally accused of committing a form of docetism when it comes to the Bible, denying its human authorship. That is basically the substance of Peter Enns' book *Inspiration and Incarnation*. The trouble is that he appears to fall off the horse on the other side, so emphasising the human origin of the Bible that he denies its divine origin. He says to Christians "do not expect more from the Bible than you would of Jesus" (i.e. he was fully immersed in his time and culture) but he also needs to add "and do not expect less."

The Bible Tells Me So, 243.

So when you hear someone talking up the humanity of Scripture, be glad – it is a wonderful truth – but, crucially, listen for an emphasis on the divine author as well.

Paul is also a favourite hunting ground. Sometimes it is the idea that Romans 1-4 is contradictory (e.g. 2:13 and 3:20 – can doers of the Law be justified or not?) or that his letters reveal that as he gets older he changes his mind about how soon Jesus will return.

Contradictions between OT books: Chalke identifies different visions of the renewed people of God in Isaiah on the one hand and Ezra and Nehemiah on the other. Isaiah imagines the nations streaming up to Jerusalem whereas Ezra and Nehemiah oppose intermarriage with the nations, concerned to maintain the purity of Israel. Or there's the question of whether God really requires sacrifice - Leviticus legislates for it, Psalm 40:6 seems to have moved on.

Going Deeper: *Metaphors matter - and you can do a lot with them*

We have already seen how the analogy of the incarnation is a limited but helpful way of thinking about the inspiration of Scripture. There are also a host of other images floating around that try to capture something of the distinctiveness of the human authors, and the diversity of Scripture. Each time though, we need to ask both what are the inherent limitations of the comparison, and how specifically are they being used to emphasise?

For example, Steve Chalke speaks of the Bible not as one book but as a library. He begins with the fact that the term 'Bible' is derived from the Greek *ta biblia* (the books); he then assumes a collection of books is the same as a library and asks what you would expect if you picked up a number of books in say, a history library. Answer: different perspectives that overlap, complement, and sometimes contradict each other; and thus the metaphor is deployed to illustrate his view of Scripture's lack of unity.

Now in a sense the Bible is a library but the comparison is really very limited. At the very least we would need to flag it up that the metaphor lacks any built-in sense of unity. The Bible is one book and many books.

For reflection – how helpful are the following? What are their relative strengths and weaknesses?

Andrew Wilson, *Unbreakable: What the Son of God Said About the Word of God* (10Publishing, 2014), 21.

Consider a jazz musician who can play all sorts of different instruments. Nobody, listening to Louis Armstrong, would ask whether the music was being made by Louis or his trumpet; everybody knows that the breath and tune come from Louis, but the instrument through which the breath passes, in order to become audible, is the trumpet. The Bible writers, if you like, are the instruments of revelation – a trumpet here, an oboe there, a saxophone here – and they all make different sounds. But the musician, the skilled artist who fills them all with his breath and ensures the tune is played correctly, is the Holy Spirit. That's kind of how inspiration works.

Letter To Marcellinus 'On The Interpretation Of The Psalms'

Or what about Athanasius' fruity image of the books of the Bible: "Each of these books, you see, is like a garden which grows one special kind of fruit," or look out for Warfield's image of stained glass in the excerpt from his article on 'Inspiration' later in this issue. What do these capture? How are they limited? How is Warfield aware that the window image can be misused?

Contradictions between NT books: We could cite here apparent contradictions between the gospels – e.g. the question of when Jesus cleansed the temple, at the start of his ministry (John 2) or at the end (Matthew 21, Mark 13, Luke 19), or the question of whether we are justified by faith (Romans 4) or by works (James 2).

Contradictions between OT and NT: Steve Chalke points to the way Jesus re-interprets the Sabbath commands. Peter Enns thinks Paul has had do some interpretive gymnastics to make space in the Bible's story for a law-free Gentile church:

> *Paul had to reimagine his Scripture, transforming it from a local and ethnic story into a universal story around Jesus. Paul even wound up declaring parts of Israel's story null and void. If you are expecting Paul to read the Bible like it was set in stone, you will find yourself getting pretty nervous. For Paul, now that Jesus has come, the Bible was more like clay to be molded*

Peter Enns, *The Bible Tells Me So*, 214.

Now, if that is the diversity being discussed, how to respond?

1. This is one of the oldest objections to the Bible and many of these issues have been well-answered in the past. The early church very quickly set about creating harmonies of the gospels precisely because they met suggestions of contradiction and wanted to demonstrate that the Gospels do not in fact contradict each other. At the very least that means we should be suspicious of anyone who says "Hey everyone, I've just realised there's a problem here!"

2. Many people simply assume the Bible is inconsistent and so it is usually worth just asking them to name some specific examples. Often they cannot.

3. A good number of these issues (e.g. the application of the Sabbath or the abolition of the food laws) are resolved when a basic biblical theology is in place. The best way to defend God's people then is to teach them how to read the Bible within the flow of salvation history.

4. Asking how the biblical authors treated one another is helpful. Where authors quote or refer to one another there is every impression that they express agreement with and respect towards one another. Paul thinks Peter and James agreed with him about the nature of the gospel (Gal 2:1-10) and Peter likewise speaks warmly of "our dear brother" Paul, referring to his letters as Scripture (2 Pet 3:15-16). Likewise, NT authors hardly treated the OT as clay to be "molded". Jesus' arrival was surprising and unexpected in many ways and yet the consistent NT argument is that it was nonetheless "according to the Scriptures." When NT authors thought of the OT they did not see it as something they were free to reshape but rather,

It seems both a matter of fact and part of the biblical authors' intent that their engagement with the Old Testament is at least as much a function of the text's own agency in terms of its (divine) **claim and impact on them**, rather than merely of their 'use' of it. Could one say that they speak as they do because they are thunderstruck by the pressure that Scripture **as a hermeneutical Other** exerts on their own view of things?

Markus Bockmuehl, quoted in Richard B. Hays, *Reading Backwards: Figural Christology and the Fourfold Gospel Witness* (Waco: Baylor University Press, 2014), x, emphasis original.

Put simply, they were shaped by the OT. They did not reshape it.

5. It is worth being alert to the ways in which contradictions are highlighted in order to justify the idea that the Bible is simply a conversation or a progressively evolving ethical journey. Again, it should strike us as improbable, to say the least, that our twenty-first century values should turn out to be the climax of humanity's moral journey.

See the excerpt from Strange and Ovey, *Confident: Why We Can Trust the Bible*, on pages 54-57.

6. We need to be aware that sometimes arguments about the diversity of the Bible or its interpretation are being used to avoid making ethical judgments. In particular, as we have seen this is a dynamic in the debate about homosexuality. For this reason we would do well to recover a doctrine of the clarity of Scripture. God has spoken, he does not contradict himself, and the fact that some Christians take another view does not necessarily make our reading of Scripture provisional or doubtful.

On which, see Mark D. Thompson, *A Clear and Present Word: The Clarity of Scripture*, New Studies in Biblical Theology (Nottingham: IVP, 2006).

7. Perhaps I should have put this first. The Bible *is* diverse. We actually need to take hold of this and not get so defensive that we flatten everything out.

For example, Isaiah and Ezra/Nehemiah both have something important to teach us about the people God is saving for himself – they will be a multinational people (Isaiah) and they will be a purified people, a holy people (Ezra/Nehemiah). These are different but complementary perspectives. It is both/and.

Or take that 'contradiction' in John. We do not need to accept Ehrman's suggestion that this reveals the version of John's Gospel we have is a cut-and-paste job from several different sources, but nor do we just want to spend all our time trying to resolve it as if this is just a bit of a mess John has left us to tidy up. Rather, he did it on purpose, and it is a window into the way John wants to teach us that we should not miss. Look through his Gospel and this kind of thing is everywhere. Has Jesus come to judge the world? John 9:39 says no, 12:47 says yes. Do people know where he has come from? John 7:28 says yes, 8:14 says no. The point is that these are questions that take some thinking about. There is a yes and no quality to them and John wants us to pause and ponder that.

I am grateful to Peter J. Williams for sharing the list of examples he compiled.

In various ways then the Bible offers us countless perspectives on the same God and his one plan of salvation. We need to defend the unity but we also need to celebrate the diversity.

On this theme, see Strange and Ovey, *Confident: Why We Can Trust the Bible*, chap. 4.

Conclusion

Defend and celebrate. As we have seen, the Bible is under attack, even from those who claim to champion it. In such a context, a necessary part of our pastoral and evangelistic task will be to defend and celebrate the Bible. Indeed, in many ways we have been arguing that we can best defend the Bible by celebrating it, rejoicing in the way in which comes to us: as God's perfectly true word, given through human authors, expressing truth in diverse ways and addressed to concrete historical situations. Our hope, in closing, is that the rest of this issue of Primer will equip us more and more to defend and celebrate, so that in all things we his people might be as true to God's word as he is. P

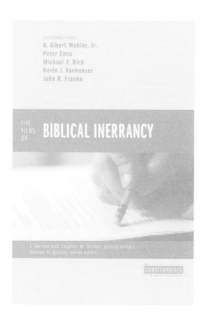

An extended review of *Five Views on Biblical Inerrancy* edited by J Merrick & Stephen M Garrett.

MAKE NO MISTAKE

by John Stevens

As David Bebbington made clear in his famous 'quadrilateral' definition of evangelicalism, evangelicals have been historically associated with a high view of the authority of Scripture. They are inherently "biblicist" and regard the Scriptures as God's full, final and sufficient revelation, and an utterly reliable guide to truth and salvation. Evangelical doctrinal statements almost invariably state their commitment to the authority and truthfulness of Scripture, although the language in which this is expressed may vary. Ever since the Enlightenment, evangelicals have defended the accuracy and truthfulness of the Bible against the onslaughts of modernism and liberalism, which have taught that it is ultimately a human book filled with mistakes and errors that vitiate its complete trustworthiness. In particular questions have been raised as to the Bible's factual accuracy regarding matters of history and science.

In the UK the truth and trustworthiness of Scripture has most commonly been asserted by evangelicals by utilising the terminology of "infallibility," which has been defined by Michael Bird as meaning that "the biblical teachings are true and without falsehood in all that they affirm, with specific reference to God's revelation of himself as Saviour." In the US the terminology of "inerrancy" has been predominant, which encapsulates the factual accuracy of the biblical record.

The high point of the development and definition of inerrancy is the *Chicago Statement on Biblical Inerrancy* (CSBI), which was signed by over 300 noted evangelical scholars in 1978. The majority of these scholars were American, though there were a small number from the UK, including J I Packer and John Wenham. Whilst the doctrine of inerrancy is often assumed by critics to require a flat and literalistic approach to the Bible, in fact the CSBI is more subtle and nuanced in its understanding of the truthfulness of the Bible, and recognises the importance of different biblical genres and appropriate hermeneutics to determine the meaning of the text.

Bebbington identifies four (hence 'quadrilateral') special marks of evangelicalism: "*conversionism*, the belief that lives need to be changed; *activism*, the expression of the gospel in effort; *biblicism*, a particular regard for the Bible; and what may be termed *crucicentrism*, a stress on the sacrifice of Christ on the cross. Together they form a quadrilateral of priorities that is the basis of evangelicalism." *Evangelicalism in Modern Britain: A History from the 1730s to the 1980s* (London: Routledge, 1989), 7.

Today there is considerable confusion amongst evangelicals about the value of inerrancy as a descriptor of biblical authority, and especially whether it ought to serve as a boundary marker of authentic biblical faith. A commitment to inerrancy is perceived by some to be fundamentalist, doctrinaire, obscurant and intolerant. Whilst it has never been the case that all self-professed evangelicals have held to the doctrine of inerrancy, nor that all inerrantists have agreed what the doctrine requires, the decline of classic liberalism and inexorable rise of open-evangelicalism, with its postmodern approaches to truth and Scripture, makes it essential to reconsider how we are to understand the authority of Scripture.

In the light of the importance of this doctrine it is to be welcomed that Zondervan have addressed inerrancy in their well-established *Counterpoints* series. Published in 2013, *Five Views on Biblical Inerrancy* draws together five leading contemporary theologians to discuss the meaning and relevance of inerrancy, as defined in the CSBI, for evangelicals today. Whilst they are all scholars of distinction they write in a way that is accessible to ordinary readers. Albert Mohler and Kevin Vanhoozer defend inerrancy, although Vanhoozer ultimately prefers the term infallibility because he believes that, properly understood, it encompasses all that is meant by inerrancy while also affirming that Scripture perfectly accomplishes all that God intends it to accomplish. Peter Enns and John Franke deny inerrancy, and hence this review will give less consideration to their views. Michael Bird purports to defend the substance of inerrancy, but prefers the term infallibility. His contribution is the most relevant for conservative evangelicals as it most fully explores the boundary between inerrancy and infallibility as rival conceptions of biblical truthfulness and authority.

Each contributor sets out their position, which is then critiqued by the others. Whilst this encourages dialogue it makes it more difficult to discern the contours of the doctrine systematically, and the contributors gradually sharpen and nuance their understanding as they interact with each other. Each author applies their understanding of inerrancy to three test cases which are thought to be problematic: The historical accuracy of the fall of Jericho (Joshua 6); The apparent contradiction between Paul's report of his encounter with Jesus on the Damascus Road (Acts 9:7 & 22:9); and the tension between God's command that the Israelites kill the Canaanites in the Old Testament and Jesus' commands to love our enemies in the Sermon on the Mount (Deut 20:16-17; Matt 5:43-48).

The discussion of inerrancy in this book is of crucial importance for contemporary evangelicals. It is essential that we understand both what inerrancy means, and why this doctrine is of vital important to the health of the church and the work of the gospel. In this article I will attempt to systematise the key issues regarding inerrancy that emerge from the debate that takes place in this book.

WHAT IS INERRANCY?

The essence of inerrancy is the conviction that the Bible is true in everything that it asserts. It is not simply a book of spiritual or religious truth, but is an accurate record of what happened in history and a truthful description of the nature of the world in which we live. Inerrancy asserts that there is a fundamental correspondence between the record of Scripture and reality. This is well stated in the CSBI:

Being wholly and verbally God-given, Scripture is without error or fault in all its teaching, no less in what it states about God's acts in creation, about the events of world history, and about its own literary origins under God, than in its witness to God's saving grace in individual lives.

If follows that if the Bible reports that the walls of Jericho fell when the Israelites blew their trumpets, then this really happened in space-time history. Likewise the account of the conquest of the Promised Land is not figurative, fictional or symbolic.

This commitment to the factual historicity of the Bible is asserted and defended most strongly by Mohler and Vanhoozer. Enns and Franke reinforce this understanding of inerrancy by their very rejection of it. Enns regards large sections of the Old Testament as fiction. In his view the fall of Jericho is "mythologised history" which is illustrative rather than actual. In this he is reminiscent of traditional liberalism. Franke adopts a postmodern approach and regards the accuracy or otherwise of the biblical record as inaccessible and unprovable, hence rendering inerrancy irrelevant as a doctrine.

The outright rejection of inerrancy by Enns and Franke means that it is Bird who most subtly probes the distinction between inerrancy and infallibility, and who critiques the CSBI whilst wishing to hold to a high view of Scripture. He strongly affirms the truthfulness and trustworthiness of the biblical record, but prefers the terminology of infallibility. In his view the Bible is intended to impart knowledge of God as Creator and Redeemer, and in this regard it is completely true in all it says. He prefers a "substantive historicity" of the biblical record rather than a strict accuracy, pointing to discrepancies in the accounts of the life and ministry of Jesus. He regards these as "incidental details" which are of minor significance, as for example whether Jesus healed a blind man on the way to Jericho (Luke) or leaving the city (Matthew and Mark).

Bird's willingness to accept a measure of imprecision and rearrangement by the story tellers highlights the key difference between infallibility and inerrancy. However as Mohler and Vanhoozer explain, inerrancy as defined by the CBSI allows for the presence of such "discrepancies" in the Bible without limiting the perfect trustworthiness of biblical revelation to matters of faith and doctrine.

It is also important to note that all those who hold to the doctrine of inerrancy readily acknowledge that the Scriptures we have in our hands today are not, in fact, entirely inerrant. The CSBI affirms that only the "autographic text of Scripture" is inspired by God, but denies that "any essential element of the Christian faith is affected by the absence of the autographs" and further denies that "this absence renders the assertion of biblical inerrancy invalid or irrelevant." Everyone acknowledges that the Bible we possess contains copying errors and unresolved discrepancies.

WHAT DOES INERRANCY DEMAND?

Although inerrancy asserts the factual truthfulness of Scripture, it is all too easy to assume that a commitment to inerrancy necessitates acceptance of other specific doctrinal positions. This occurs because inerrancy has tended to be confused with Christian fundamentalism, which characteristically adopts a flat and literalistic hermeneutic for biblical interpretation. Many people therefore assume, for example, that inerrancy requires acceptance of a young earth creationist view that the world was created in six literal 24-hour days some 6,000 years ago. The formal authority of the Bible as a whole is therefore conflated with acceptance of specific interpretations of the Scriptures.

This issue is helpfully addressed in the essays, especially by Vanhoozer who argues for what he calls a "well-versed" inerrancy that takes proper account of the nature of the biblical literature.

Inerrancy must be coupled with appropriate "literate interpretation." It follows that each biblical text must be appropriately interpreted according to its canonical function and literary genre. The Bible itself clearly uses literary devices such as poetry, metaphor, generalisation, symbol, exaggeration and hyperbole. It follows from this that inerrancy, properly understood, does not demand a literalistic interpretation of every biblical passage.

It may come as a surprise to both advocates and opponents of inerrancy that the CBSI acknowledges that "the text of Scripture is to be interpreted by grammatico-historical exegesis, taking into account its literary form and devices." A significant case in point is the creation narrative. At first glance the CSBI might appear to demand a literal six-day creation. As has been noted, it states that the Bible is without fault and error in "what it states about God's acts in creation." Article XII specifically denies that inerrancy is excluded from "the fields of history and science," and further denies that "scientific hypotheses about earth history may properly be used to overturn the teaching of Scripture on creation and flood." Whilst many inerrantists are also young-earth creationists, as were most of the framers of the CSBI, Mohler makes clear in his response to the articles of Vanhoozer and Bird that this is not a position required by inerrancy per se. Some of the framers of the CSBI were not young earth creationists, yet they were able to sign. Eschatology provides another example. Dispensationalism is ultimately driven by a literalistic hermeneutic, whereas a- and post-millennialism are dependent on a metaphorical or typological interpretation of key texts. However advocates of these very different eschatological schemes are vociferous defenders of inerrancy, and signatories to the CSBI.

Whilst Enns and Franke regard a lack of exact correspondence between reality and the biblical record as fatal for inerrancy, Mohler, Vanhoozer and Bird each recognise that apparent contradictions may be resolved by proper interpretation. The Bible is not a collection of raw facts and data, but an interpretation of that data. The authorial intent of both the human writer and the divine inspirer must be discerned by proper interpretation of the text. Differing interpretations are to be assessed and judged by the interpretative methods employed, not merely by the playing of a trump card of inerrancy and literalism.

The confusion of issues of inerrancy and interpretation is readily apparent from one of the supposed "test" cases utilised in the book. The alleged contradiction between the command of God to exterminate the Canaanite inhabitants of the Promised Land and the command of Jesus to love our enemies is essentially an issue of interpretation, and susceptible to a relatively straightforward resolution if proper account is taken of the salvation historical context of each text. It would of course be an issue of inerrancy if, as Enns believes, the conquest of Canaan never took place as described in the Old Testament record. However, presuming that the events recorded took place, the resolution lies in the application of biblical theology to assess the context and abiding relevance of the two commands. The command to the Israelites to exterminate the Canaanites was a command for that moment of salvation history, which was justified as the execution of God's judgement for their sin. Jesus' command reflects the new era of salvation history he inaugurated, in which our conquest of our enemies is through the gospel not force of arms, and we are not required to execute temporal judgement in the present. Rather the conquest of Canaan points typologically ahead to the judgement that Jesus and his people will execute when he returns in glory to claim the earth for himself. This approach is entirely consistent with the CSBI, which recognises that "God's revelation within Holy Scriptures was progressive," such that later revelation may fulfil earlier revelation, without contradicting or correcting it.

It is therefore vitally important that we distinguish between issues of inerrancy and interpretation. Robert Gundry, for example, famously argued that the birth narratives of Matthew's gospel were midrash, and ought not therefore to be taken as historically accurate. In and

Midrash is a slippery term that gets defined in different ways, but here it refers to a Jewish technique or genre of biblical interpretation which is less concerned with historical accuracy.

of itself this is not a direct rejection of biblical inerrancy. Rather, as most conservative evangelical commentators argue, it is a false interpretation of the text, ascribing the wrong genre category to a section of Scripture that is clearly presented as historical. The key question in such cases is therefore whether the text in question was intended to be treated as historical or scientifically accurate.

It is too easy to condemn false teaching and false teachers on the grounds that they have denied inerrancy, rather than to tackle their incorrect interpretations on their own terms. Inerrancy ought not to be the argument of first resort against unjustifiable interpretations. For example, the views of self-proclaimed evangelicals who wish to affirm God's acceptance of committed homosexual relationships are liable to be dismissed too simplistically on the grounds that they reject inerrancy and biblical authority, rather than by exposing the faulty interpretative methodology that underlies their conclusions. Whilst some proponents of same-sex relationships do regard the Bible as a human book that is flawed and mistaken about homosexuality, others mount a more sophisticated argument that the Bible does not have loving same-sex relationships in view when it condemns homosexuality, or alternatively that there is a discernible trajectory towards liberation and equality in the Bible as a whole that would logically culminate in the acceptance of homosexual relationships. Where such arguments are mounted it is necessary to demonstrate that the interpretation itself is untenable, not just that the interpretation amounts to a rejection of biblical authority. The first response is not an appeal to the doctrine of inerrancy, but to the consistent condemnation in the Bible of all sexual activity outside heterosexual marriage, the specific condemnation of homosexual practice at every stage of salvation history, and the absence of any reference anywhere that would suggest a positive attitude towards homosexuality.

These illustrations are a reminder of the need to maintain a distinction between issues of authority and interpretation. Relying on the doctrine of inerrancy alone to refute false teaching, rather than engaging with the direct interpretative issues themselves, may defend orthodox beliefs in the short term, but leave them open to rejection by subsequent generations who lack the categories to take them on their own merits.

Inerrancy alone cannot resolve interpretative debates. Specific interpretations of biblical texts ought to be rejected, and regarded as beyond the boundaries of evangelicalism, if they are patently unsustainable and unjustified, irrespective of their advocates' claims to respect biblical authority. Interpretations that are novel, have no support in the history of evangelicalism, require special pleading to overcome the apparent meaning of the words used, are contrary to each and every other biblical text, or which deny the long-established doctrinal formulations of the historic creeds and the Reformation "Solas," must be rejected even if accompanied by a claim to uphold inerrancy.

That is, the Apostles' Creed, along with the Nicene and Athanasian creeds.

Sola scriptura (Scripture alone), *solus Christus* (saved by Christ alone) *sola gratia* (by grace alone) *sola fide* (and by faith alone), *soli deo gloria* (to the glory of God alone).

WHAT IS AN ERROR?

A preliminary question that arises in relation to inerrancy, and which sadly is not very clearly addressed in the book, is what precisely is meant by an "error." How far should we expect the biblical text to conform to modern conventions of accuracy and precision? As has already been noted, there is a recognition by most inerrantists that the Bible authors may use approximations, generalisations and hyperbole. Poetic language does not necessarily seek to speak about the world in scientifically accurate ways. The scandal of historical particularity means that God's revelation was given at specific moments of human history and in the forms that were prevalent at those times, including the use of human languages and literary forms.

As evangelicals have long recognised, God has to some extent accommodated his revelation anthropomorphically. For example, whilst the Bible speaks of God as having the attributes of a human body – whether feet, hands, eyes, ears or mouth – it also asserts that he is a spiritual being. Such language is clearly intended to be metaphorical rather than to give an accurate scientific description of God's anatomy. The necessity of accommodation allows for the possibility that the Bible will speak of creation and the natural world using the categories of the prevailing cosmologies of the Ancient Near East, albeit critiquing them and their polytheistic and dualistic worldview. Similarly the Bible might be expected to utilise human observations of the natural world, for example of the sun travelling around the earth, and to adopt ancient classifications of animal biology. The historical situatedness of Scripture means that these are not "errors" as such, but highlight the fact that the Bible does not profess to be a modern scientific textbook. It is equally well recognised that the Bible does not record the *ipsissima verba* of Jesus, so that the exact words that he uses vary between different gospel accounts of identical incidents. The kind of verbal precision expected and demanded in our contemporary world of sound and video recording is simply not appropriate for the Bible.

Ipsissima verba means the very words of Jesus. Sometimes this is contrasted with the idea that in the gospels we have the *ipsissima vox* (the very voice) of Jesus. That is, we hear his voice through the translation and rephrasing of the gospel authors. His voice comes through even though we don't know his exact original words.

It is therefore inevitable that we cannot apply the modern definition of "error" simplistically to the Bible, and all the authors in the book recognise this difficulty, even those who are the most ardent defenders of inerrancy. However, there is a fundamental difference between recognising that the biological classification of the rabbit was perceived differently in ancient times and concluding, as Enns does, that large swathes of the Old Testament narrative is simply made up for theological reasons.

Bird attempts a mediating position of "substantive accuracy" to explain many apparent discrepancies in the biblical accounts. He approaches the alleged discrepancy between the report of Paul's conversion in Acts 9:7 and Acts 22:9 (as to whether Paul's companions heard or saw what happened) by considering the cultural conventions of accuracy at the time:

I doubt that either Luke or his readers were quite so befuddled with such details, as ancient historians were more concerned with reporting the gist of events than with describing the minutiae with pinpoint precision. Ancient historians were storytellers, not modern journalists, so naturally they were given to creativity in their narratives and filled in the gaps on details where necessary ... Luke's narration is flexible on the details simply because the genre in which he was writing allowed him to be so without any discredit to his reputation for reliability. The use of such genres in biblical revelation indicates that the truthfulness of revelation is not tied to incidental details.

In his estimation such apparent discrepancies in the details of reportage are "innocuous." However, this approach seems to give too much away and to highlight once again the difference between infallibility and inerrancy as descriptors of biblical authority.

Whilst the genre of narrative in the New Testament may not require "pinpoint precision" in details, this is not the same as claiming that the biblical authors were mere storytellers who felt free to improvise their accounts and pad them out with their own fictive material. This would be to reduce the biblical text to the level of a contemporary docu-drama, or an imagined historical re-enactment. It would be impossible to distinguish which elements of the text are authentic and trustworthy and which are mere literary embellishment.

Bird's argument at this point tends to undermine his assertion that infallibility is "not a retreatist position" and to confirm the critique of inerrantists that it is, in his words, "too soft and not assertive enough." Whilst Bird clearly stands within the evangelical camp, his arguments here seem to give too much away and to open the door to liberal and postmodern critique of the traditional doctrine of Scripture.

Having said this, as was noted above, most inerrantists readily acknowledge that the Bible includes approximations and generalisations. The book is a helpful reminder that the doctrine of inerrancy should not be pushed to require the Scriptures to conform to exacting modern standards of historiography or scientific writing. Calvin himself recognised this, writing in his *Commentary on Luke 11:12*: "We know that the Evangelists were not very exact as to the order of dates, or even in detailing minutely everything that Christ did or said." However Enns and Franke go much further than this, and believe that the biblical authors were knowingly passing off falsehoods as truth.

The CSBI helpfully clarifies the proper limits of inerrancy:

> *We deny that it is proper to evaluate Scripture according to standards of truth and error that are alien to its usage or purpose. We further deny that inerrancy is negated by biblical phenomena such as a lack of modern technical precision, irregularities of grammar or spelling, observational descriptions of nature, the reporting of falsehoods, the use of hyperbole and round numbers, the topical arrangement of material, variant selections of material in parallel accounts, or by the free use of citations.*

If these caveats are taken into account, qualifying a flat and literalistic conception of inerrancy, then many of the alleged minor discrepancies in the Bible's rapportage of events are explicable on the basis of the prevailing cultural conventions of truthfulness and accuracy.

HOW DO WE KNOW THAT THE BIBLE IS INERRANT?

Whilst at many points the evidence of history and science confirm the veracity of the biblical record, this is not proof of inerrancy nor the basis of inerrancy. Unless every potential factual detail was able to be externally verified and confirmed it would be impossible to establish inerrancy. Inerrancy may be disproved by clear and incontrovertible evidence of error, but it cannot be positively established by external proof. The most that external evidence can achieve is to give rational and reasonable grounds for believing that the Bible is inerrant. As the two authors who advocate inerrancy make clear, the basis for inerrancy is located in the very character of God.

The Scriptures testify that they are the word of God inspired by his Spirit and written through human authors. It follows as a matter of necessity that the Scripture will thus be inerrant because God is faithful and does not lie. He is omniscient and there is nothing that he does not know with perfect accuracy. His sovereign rule over the whole of creation and free human actions ensures that every single word of the original autographs is exactly as he wanted it to be. If the true God is indeed the God of the Bible then inerrancy is the inevitable outcome of inspiration. The CSBI makes clear that the property of inerrancy is the result of the fact that the Scripture was "wholly and verbally God-given." Vanhoozer refers approvingly to the recent work of Tim Ward, who has applied speech-act theory to the doctrine of biblical inspiration, and who shows that inerrancy is a logical implication of the character of God and his revelation of himself.

Whilst this might seem to be a circular argument, it is no more so than the arguments against the inerrancy of Scripture, which presuppose an objective and unbiased position from which to stand in judgement over Scripture, and assert an omniscience about the facts of history and science from which to critique the biblical record. Franke is quite right to note that inerrancy is thus an aspect of foundationalism, which as a postmodernist he regards as discredited. In practice the vast majority of inerrantists do not come to faith in Jesus as a result of any prior convictions about the inerrancy of the Scriptures. Rather they come to faith in the inerrancy of the Scriptures because they have come to faith in Jesus, and they discover that he affirms that they are indeed inerrant.

Ultimately evangelicals have always based their faith in the inerrancy of the Bible on the witness of the Spirit to the truth of the Scriptures, which results in their self-attestation. This may be bolstered by external evidence confirming their confidence, and the absence of categorical evidence undermining it, but it is not founded epistemologically on such empirical external data. This would be to acknowledge a greater authority than God and the Scriptures themselves, namely human discovery and reason. It follows that Christians who seek to "prove" the inerrancy of the Scriptures claim too much for their efforts, and their over-confidence in their ability to do so may lead to a discrediting of the doctrine.

If inerrancy is rooted in the character of God and nature of the Scriptures, it follows that it is reasonable to suspend judgement when external evidence appears to contradict the biblical text. This is especially evident in the book in regard to the historicity or otherwise of the fall of Jericho. Enns relies on contemporary archaeological theory to discredit the truthfulness of the account. However Mohler and Vanhoozer point to alternative archaeological theories that call the prevailing consensus into question, and to the way in which the data concerning Jericho has been interpreted differently over the past century or so. Since archaeological theories change, and new evidence may be discovered, they assert that there is no compelling reason to reject the biblical account.

THE BASIS FOR INERRANCY IS LOCATED IN THE VERY CHARACTER OF GOD.

In the same way inerrantists acknowledge the presence of unresolved discrepancies and contradictions in the biblical texts as we have them, but this does not lead them to abandon inerrancy. They trust that new evidence or new manuscripts may come to light that will satisfactorily resolve them in future, and they can point to well-known instances where this has occurred. In some cases the apparent discrepancies and contradictions may be impossible to resolve because new evidence never comes to light, but this does not mean that the Bible as originally given was in error. Our lack of omniscience means that we have to exercise a high degree of epistemological humility about our knowledge of reality. We have far better reasons for trusting the inerrancy of the Scriptures than the infallibility of contemporary science, archaeology or history. The most we can establish from external evidence is that inerrancy is not an irrational doctrine.

CONCLUSION

Overall this book is a helpful overview of the doctrine of inerrancy as understood by its contemporary proponents and opponents. Mohler and Vanhoozer are to be thanked for their able defence of inerrancy, and for stating so clearly and repeatedly that inerrancy does not demand beliefs that its most vocal critics find objectionable, such as a young earth creationism, nor does it refuse to take account of the literary and historical context of biblical texts. It turns out that the CBSI, whilst written in an American modernist milieu that seems slightly dated, is altogether more sophisticated and subtle than its detractors suggest or presume. It remains the best statement of inerrancy, and of the necessary implications of this doctrine.

Enns and Franke both profess to be evangelical but their contributions reveal how shaky Christian faith will become if the truthfulness of the Scriptures is rejected. Their honest contributions make abundantly clear what is at stake if the doctrine of inerrancy is rejected. If God's mighty acts of redemption in history, such as the exodus and the conquest of the promised land, did not really happen but are fictionalised myth, then the God of the Bible does not exist.

Bird prefers the language of *infallibility* over *inerrancy*, largely because he is allergic to the American fundamentalist connotations that are often associated with inerrancy, and attempts to argue that they are virtually identical in practice. However his focus on the substantive truth of the Scriptures, whilst allowing that some details may be fictive or imaginary, gives too much away. As soon as it is conceded that at some points the Scriptures are a fictive human narrative, albeit in the context of substantive truth, then the question arises as to how to differentiate the trustworthy truth from the literary flourishes in the text. Having said this, his contribution, together with that of Vanhoozer, is a helpful reminder that we must not pit inerrancy against infallibility. Rather we should assert and affirm both. God has a purpose to achieve in the Scriptures, revealing himself and the way of salvation (cf. 2 Tim 3:15-17) and the Scriptures perfectly accomplish this purpose. Adding infallibility alongside inerrancy prevents the doctrine becoming merely abstract, theoretical or defensive.

In the end the Christian faith stands or falls with the truthfulness of the Bible. You cannot trust in Jesus whilst simultaneously rejecting Jesus' own convictions, affirmation and teaching about the absolute truthfulness of the Bible. Time and again he confirms details of the historical narrative of the Old Testament and declares it to be the word of his Father. He bases his life and ministry on its veracity and reliability. Inerrancy might be an off-putting, technical and misunderstood term, but it remains the best way of articulating the total truthfulness of Scripture, which is the word from God expressed in divinely inspired human words. It encapsulates the way in which the Bible understands itself, and the way in which Jesus understood the Bible. It states in a negative way the inevitable implications of the doctrines of revelation and inspiration. The nuanced way in which inerrancy is explained in the CSBI allows for the literary character of the Bible to be fully taken into account, and prevents a crass literalism from discrediting the doctrine.

Inerrancy is thus a crucial doctrine that the church must believe and defend. I am thankful that FIEC, among others, has chosen to take its stand not just on the doctrine of infallibility but also on that of inerrancy. As our Doctrinal Basis states, we believe that the Bible is "without error and fully reliable in fact and doctrine." Whether we like the terminology of inerrancy or not, the truth it seeks to articulate about the Bible is essential to our faith, salvation and gospel ministry. We reject it at our peril. P

INSPIRATION

An excerpt from B.B. Warfield's 1915 article with an introduction and annotations by Fred Zaspel.

Portrait: *Benjamin Breckinridge Warfield* by Ernest Ludvig Ipsen (Special Collections, Princeton Theological Seminary Library)

The essay that follows is just a portion of an article written by B.B. Warfield in 1915 for the famous multi-volume work, International Standard Bible Encyclopedia – "ISBE" as it came to be known. Warfield had written many hundreds of pages over the years dedicated to the subject of *Inspiration*, or some aspect of it, and coming late in his career this article is significant as his final comprehensive and definitive statement on the doctrine.

The particular passage we will consider below is preceded by an examination of three primary biblical passages on the doctrine of inspiration. The first is **2 Timothy 3:15-16**

> *... from childhood you have been acquainted with the sacred writings, which are able to make you wise for salvation through faith in Christ Jesus. All Scripture is breathed out by God and profitable for teaching, for reproof, for correction, and for training in righteousness. (ESV)*

Here the apostle Paul identifies "Scripture" (v.16) as "sacred writings" (v.15), a technical term nowhere else used in the NT but found in other Jewish writings to designate those writings given from God and constituting his Law. That is, the very terminology Paul uses to designate the Bible reflects his conviction that it is divinely given and divinely authoritative.

Further, the apostle affirms that Scripture is "God-breathed," his own spoken word – "the product of the creative breath of God," as Warfield puts it.

Paul could not have stated more emphatically than he does here that Scripture is God's very own word and that in reading it we must receive it as from God himself.

In **2 Peter 1:19-21** the apostle Peter clarifies Paul's affirmation, specifying for us just how God's Word came to us.

> *And we have the prophetic word more fully confirmed, to which you will do well to pay attention as to a lamp shining in a dark place, until the day dawns and the morning star rises in your hearts, knowing this first of all, that no prophecy of Scripture comes from someone's own interpretation. For no prophecy was ever produced by the will of man, but men spoke from God as they were carried along by the Holy Spirit. (ESV)*

That is, Scripture did not arise in anything human but, rather, God's inspired spokesmen spoke and wrote "as they were carried along by the Holy Spirit." Again the divine origin of Scripture is what is emphasized. Any idea of the human origin of Scripture is emphatically denied, and its divine origin is just as emphatically affirmed. The biblical writers spoke and wrote as they were "taken up and carried along" by the Spirit of God. In this sense their writings are rightly designated "prophetic" or "prophecy," a designation itself asserting that the biblical writers were divine spokesmen. Warfield emphasizes in all this that the biblical writers were the instrumentality God used in giving his Word to us.

It is important to notice the conclusion that Peter draws from this fact. Precisely because Scripture is of divine origin, it is "more fully confirmed," or "more sure." Scripture is trustworthy because it is the Word of God.

The third passage Warfield offers is **John 10:33-35**.

The Jews answered him, "It is not for a good work that we are going to stone you but for blasphemy, because you, being a man, make yourself God." Jesus answered them, "Is it not written in your Law, 'I said, you are gods'? If he called them gods to whom the word of God came – and Scripture cannot be broken – do you say of him whom the Father consecrated and sent into the world, 'You are blaspheming,' because I said, 'I am the Son of God'?" (ESV)

Here Jesus silences his opponents with a seeming technicality: since the Scripture itself uses the term "gods" of human judges (Ps. 82:6), then they have little ground for their objection to his affirmation that he is "the Son of God." But what is important here for Warfield, first, is that Jesus ends the discussion with a mere citation of Scripture as God's authoritative Word. Clearly, for Jesus, Scripture speaks with final, divine authority.

But most important is Jesus' affirmation, "Scripture cannot be broken." Because it is God's very own word, Scripture is supremely authoritative and cannot fail at any point. And this Jesus affirms not only of the relatively obscure statement of Psalm 82:6 but of "Scripture" generally.

Warfield's point in all this is to demonstrate that in the view of Jesus and the apostles Scripture is divinely given, divinely authoritative, and divinely trustworthy. Many other passages could be shown to provide or reflect the same conviction, but these three Warfield chooses as primary summary statements of the doctrine. Having established the teaching of these passages, then, he is able to address various aspects of the doctrine. In particular, he addresses what he calls the "human element of Scripture"...

The following is excerpted from B.B. Warfield, 'Inspiration' in *The International Standard Bible Encyclopedia* (Grand Rapids: Eerdmans, 1939).

THE HUMAN ELEMENT IN SCRIPTURE

That the Scriptures are throughout a Divine book, created by the Divine energy and speaking in their every part with Divine authority directly to the heart of the readers, is the fundamental fact concerning them which is witnessed by Christ and the sacred writers to whom we owe the New Testament. But the strength and constancy with which they bear witness to this primary fact do not prevent their recognizing by the side of it that the Scriptures have come into being by the agency of men. It would be inexact to say that they recognize a human element in Scripture: they do not parcel Scripture out, assigning portions of it, or elements in it, respectively to God and man. In their view the whole of Scripture in all its parts and in all its elements, down to the least minutiae, in form of expression as well as in substance of teaching, is from God; but the whole of it has been given by God through the instrumentality of men. There is, therefore, in their view, not, indeed, a human element or ingredient in Scripture, and much less human divisions or sections of Scripture, but a human side or aspect to Scripture; and they do not fail to give full recognition to this human side or aspect. In one of the primary passages which has already been before us, their conception is given, if somewhat broad and very succinct, yet clear expression. No "prophecy," Peter tells us (2 Pet 1:21), "ever came by the will of man; but as borne by the Holy Ghost, men spake from God." Here the whole initiative is assigned to God, and such complete control of the human agents that the product is truly God's work. The men who speak in this "prophecy of scripture" speak not of themselves or out of themselves, but from "God": they speak only as they are "borne by the Holy Ghost." But it is they, after all, who speak. Scripture is the product of man, but only of man speaking from God and under such a control of the Holy Spirit as that in their speaking they are "borne" by Him. The conception obviously is that the Scriptures have been given by the instrumentality of men; and this conception finds repeated incidental expression throughout the New Testament.

It is this conception, for example, which is expressed when our Lord, quoting Ps 110, declares of its words that "David himself said in the Holy Spirit" (Mk 12:36). There is a certain emphasis here on the words being David's own words, which is due to the requirements of the argument our Lord was conducting, but which none the less sincerely represents our Lord's conception of their

In this first paragraph Warfield summarizes his view of Scripture crisply. The Bible is a "Divine Book" in that God is its primary and ultimate author. Yet it is a "human book" also in that God gave it through human "instrumentality." That is, he used men to write his Word. Scripture, then, is God's Word written by men.

This is the whole doctrine of Scripture in summary which in the following paragraphs Warfield explains and expounds more fully.

What Warfield means by this is that though the biblical writers on occasion do make pointed, summary declaration of the inspiration of Scripture (e.g., 2 Tim. 3:16; 2 Pet. 1:21), the same doctrine is reflected throughout Scripture in "incidental" ways, such that even if we lacked those more definitive summary statements we would be forced to conclude the same doctrine that they declare.

origin. They are David's own words which we find in Ps 110, therefore; but they are David's own words, spoken not of his own motion merely, but "in the Holy Spirit," that is to say — we could not better paraphrase it — "as borne by the Holy Spirit." In other words, they are "God-breathed" words and therefore authoritative in a sense above what any words of David, not spoken in the Holy Spirit, could possibly be. Generalizing the matter, we may say that the words of Scripture are conceived by our Lord and the New Testament writers as the words of their human authors when speaking "in the Holy Spirit," that is to say, by His initiative and under His controlling direction. The conception finds even more precise expression, perhaps, in such a statement as we find — it is Peter who is speaking and it is again a psalm which is cited — in Acts 1:16, "The Holy Spirit spake by the mouth of David." Here the Holy Spirit is adduced, of course, as the real author of what is said (and hence, Peter's certainty that what is said will be fulfilled); but David's mouth is expressly designated as the instrument (it is the instrumental preposition that is used) by means of which the Holy Spirit speaks the Scripture in question. He does not speak save through David's mouth. Accordingly, in Acts 4:25, "the Lord that made the heaven and earth," acting by His Holy Spirit, is declared to have spoken another psalm "through the mouth of .... David," His "servant"; and in Mt 13:35 still another psalm is adduced as "spoken through the prophet" (compare Mt 2:5). In the very act of energetically asserting the Divine origin of Scripture the human instrumentality through which it is given is constantly recognized. The New Testament writers have, therefore, no difficulty in assigning Scripture to its human authors, or in discovering in Scripture traits due to its human authorship. They freely quote it by such simple formulas as these: "Moses saith" (Rom 10:19); "Moses said" (Mt 22:24; Mk 10; Acts 3:22); "Moses writeth" (Rom 10:5); "Moses wrote" (Mk 12:19; Lk 20:28); "Isaiah .... saith" (Rom 10:20); "Isaiah said" (Jn 12:39); "Isaiah crieth" (Rom 9:27); "Isaiah hath said before" (Rom 9:29); "said Isaiah the prophet" (Jn 1:23); "did Isaiah prophesy" (Mk 7:6: Mt 15:7); "David saith" (Lk 20:42; Acts 2:25; Rom 11:9); "David said" (Mk 12:36). It is to be noted that when thus Scripture is adduced by the names of its human authors, it is a matter of complete indifference whether the words adduced are comments of these authors or direct words of God recorded by them. As the plainest words of the human authors are assigned to God as their real author, so the most express words of God, repeated by the Scriptural writers, are cited by the names of these human

Warfield often uses expressions like this to remind and emphasize that, ultimately, Scripture is from God. It is His Word, a "gift" from him to us.

writers (Mt 15:7; Mk 7:6; Rom 10:5 19, 20; compare Mk 7:10 from the Decalogue). To say that "Moses" or "David says," is evidently thus only a way of saying that "Scripture says," which is the same as to say that "God says." Such modes of citing Scripture, accordingly, carry us little beyond merely connecting the name, or perhaps we may say the individuality, of the several writers with the portions of Scripture given through each. How it was given through them is left meanwhile, if not without suggestion, yet without specific explanation. We seem safe only in inferring this much: that the gift of Scripture through its human authors took place by a process much more intimate than can be expressed by the term "dictation," and that it took place in a process in which the control of the Holy Spirit was too complete and pervasive to permit the human qualities of the secondary authors in any way to condition the purity of the product as the word of God. The Scriptures, in other words, are conceived by the writers of the New Testament as through and through God's book, in every part expressive of His mind, given through men after a fashion which does no violence to their nature as men, and constitutes the book also men's book as well as God's, in every part expressive of the mind of its human authors.

The purpose of this paragraph is to demonstrate that even the words of the human authors – words expressing their own emotions and observations – are referred to by Jesus and later biblical writers as the words of God.

ACTIVITIES OF GOD IN GIVING SCRIPTURE

If we attempt to get behind this broad statement and to obtain a more detailed conception of the activities by which God has given the Scriptures, we are thrown back upon somewhat general representations, supported by the analogy of the modes of God's working in other spheres of His operation. It is very desirable that we should free ourselves at the outset from influences arising from the current employment of the term "inspiration" to designate this process. This term is not a Biblical term and its etymological implications are not perfectly accordant with the Biblical conception of the modes of the Divine operation in giving the Scriptures. The Biblical writers do not conceive of the Scriptures as a human product breathed into by the Divine Spirit, and thus heightened in its qualities or endowed with new qualities; but as a Divine product produced through the instrumentality of men. They do not conceive of these men, by whose instrumentality Scripture is produced, as working upon their own initiative, though energized by God to greater effort and higher achievement, but as moved by the Divine initiative and borne by the irresistible power of the Spirit of God along ways of His choosing to ends

Warfield is acknowledging here simply that though we can say with confidence that Scripture comes to us from God through human instrumentality, mystery remains as to the intricacies of that process.

Warfield frequently stresses, as he does in this paragraph, that the English word "INspiration" is technically inadequate, even misleading. God did not breathe "into" the writings of men to give those writings a divine quality. Rather, Scripture is breathed OUT by God – it is his own very Word, though given through men. "Breathed out" (Greek, theopneustos) is the very word the apostle Paul uses in 2 Tim. 3:16.

If 2 Tim. 3:16 declares that all Scripture is "breathed out by God," 2 Peter 1:21 tells us HOW this was accomplished: "holy men of God spoke as they were carried along by the Holy Spirit."

of His appointment. The difference between the two conceptions may not appear great when the mind is fixed exclusively upon the nature of the resulting product. But they are differing conceptions, and look at the production of Scripture from distinct points of view — the human and the Divine; and the involved mental attitudes toward the origin of Scripture are very diverse. The term "inspiration" is too firmly fixed, in both theological and popular usage, as the technical designation of the action of God in giving the Scriptures, to be replaced; and we may be thankful that its native implications lie as close as they do to the Biblical conceptions. Meanwhile, however, it may be justly insisted that it shall receive its definition from the representations of Scripture, and not be permitted to impose upon our thought ideas of the origin of Scripture derived from an analysis of its own implications, etymological or historical. The Scriptural conception of the relation of the Divine Spirit to the human authors in the production of Scripture is better expressed by the figure of "bearing" than by the figure of "inbreathing"; and when our Biblical writers speak of the action of the Spirit of God in this relation as a breathing, they represent it as a "breathing out" of the Scriptures by the Spirit, and not a "breathing into" the Scriptures by Him.

GENERAL PROBLEM OF ORIGIN: GOD'S PART

So soon, however, as we seriously endeavor to form for ourselves a clear conception of the precise nature of the Divine action in this "breathing out" of the Scriptures — this "bearing" of the writers of the Scriptures to their appointed goal of the production of a book of Divine trustworthiness and indefectible authority — we become acutely aware of a more deeply lying and much wider problem, apart from which this one of inspiration, technically so called, cannot be profitably considered. This is the general problem of the origin of the Scriptures and the part of God in all that complex of processes by the interaction of which these books, which we call the sacred Scriptures, with all their peculiarities, and all their qualities of whatever sort, have been brought into being. For, of course, these books were not produced suddenly, by some miraculous act — handed down complete out of heaven, as the phrase goes; but, like all other products of time, are the ultimate effect of many processes cooperating through long periods. There is to be considered, for instance, the preparation of the material which forms the subject-matter of these books:

in a sacred history, say, for example, to be narrated; or in a religious experience which may serve as a norm for record; or in a logical elaboration of the contents of revelation which may be placed at the service of God's people; or in the progressive revelation of Divine truth itself, supplying their culminating contents. And there is the preparation of the men to write these books to be considered, a preparation physical, intellectual, spiritual, which must have attended them throughout their whole lives, and, indeed, must have had its beginning in their remote ancestors, and the effect of which was to bring the right men to the right places at the right times, with the right endowments, impulses, acquirements, to write just the books which were designed for them. When "inspiration," technically so called, is superinduced on lines of preparation like these, it takes on quite a different aspect from that which it bears when it is thought of as an isolated action of the Divine Spirit operating out of all relation to historical processes. Representations are sometimes made as if, when God wished to produce sacred books which would incorporate His will — a series of letters like those of Paul, for example — He was reduced to the necessity of going down to earth and painfully scrutinizing the men He found there, seeking anxiously for the one who, on the whole, promised best for His purpose; and then violently forcing the material He wished expressed through him, against his natural bent, and with as little loss from his recalcitrant characteristics as possible. Of course, nothing of the sort took place. If God wished to give His people a series of letters like Paul's, He prepared a Paul to write them, and the Paul He brought to the task was a Paul who spontaneously would write just such letters.

Warfield's point here is that though the divine act of inspiration pertains to the actual writing of Scripture, God in his all-embracing providence nonetheless prepared the biblical writers beforehand, through all their life experiences, for the task he had for them.

HOW HUMAN QUALITIES AFFECTED SCRIPTURE: PROVIDENTIAL PREPARATION

If we bear this in mind, we shall know what estimate to place upon the common representation to the effect that the human characteristics of the writers must, and in point of fact do, condition and qualify the writings produced by them, the implication being that, therefore, we cannot get from man a pure word of God. As light that passes through the colored glass of a cathedral window, we are told, is light from heaven, but is stained by the tints of the glass through which it passes; so any word of God which is passed through the mind and soul of a man must come out discolored by the personality through which it is given, and just to that degree ceases to be the pure word of God. But what if this personality has itself been formed by God into precisely the personality it is, for the express purpose of communicating to the word given through it just the coloring which it gives it? What if the colors of the stained-glass window have been designed by the architect for the express purpose of giving to the light that floods the cathedral precisely the tone and quality it receives from them? What if the word of God that comes to His people is framed by God into the word of God it is, precisely by means of the qualities of the men formed by Him for the purpose, through which it is given? When we think of God the Lord giving by His Spirit a body of authoritative Scriptures to His people, we must remember that He is the God of providence and of grace as well as of revelation and inspiration, and that He holds all the lines of preparation as fully under His direction as He does the specific operation which we call technically, in the narrow sense, by the name of "inspiration." The production of the Scriptures is, in point of fact, a long process, in the course of which numerous and very varied Divine activities are involved, providential, gracious, miraculous, all of which must be taken into account in any attempt to explain the relation of God to the production of Scripture. When they are all taken into account we can no longer wonder that the resultant Scriptures are constantly spoken of as the pure word of God. We wonder, rather, that an additional operation of God — what we call specifically "inspiration," in its technical sense — was thought necessary. Consider, for example, how a piece of sacred history — say the Book of Chronicles, or the great historical work, Gospel and Acts, of Luke — is brought to the writing. There is first of all the preparation of the history to be written: God the Lord leads the sequence of occurrences through the development He has designed for them that they may convey their lessons to His people: a "teleological" or "etiological" character is inherent in the very course of events. Then He prepares a man, by birth, training, experience, gifts of grace, and, if need be, of revelation, capable of appreciating this historical development and eager to search it out, thrilling in all his being with its lessons and bent upon making them clear and effective to others. When, then, by His providence, God sets this man to work on the writing of this history, will there not be spontaneously written by him the history which it was Divinely intended should be written? Or consider how a psalmist would be prepared to put into moving verse a piece of normative religious experience: how he would be born with just the right quality of religious

Notice that Warfield is careful to keep in mind the divine priority in the production of Scripture. Though given through men it is God's word nonetheless. The human aspect does not dominate but the divine. And if this is so, then it is no wonder that the Bible is yet "the pure word of God."

That is, all events have a cause (aitia = etiology) and a purpose (telos = teleology) that arise from God's sovereign plan.

sensibility, of parents through whom he should receive just the right hereditary bent, and from whom he should get precisely the right religious example and training, in circumstances of life in which his religious tendencies should be developed precisely on right lines; how he would be brought through just the right experiences to quicken in him the precise emotions he would be called upon to express, and finally would be placed in precisely the exigencies which would call out their expression. Or consider the providential preparation of a writer of a didactic epistle — by means of which he should be given the intellectual breadth and acuteness, and be trained in habitudes of reasoning, and placed in the situations which would call out precisely the argumentative presentation of Christian truth which was required of him. When we give due place in our thoughts to the universality of the providential government of God, to the minuteness and completeness of its sway, and to its invariable efficacy, we may be inclined to ask what is needed beyond this mere providential government to secure the production of sacred books which should be in every detail absolutely accordant with the Divine will.

"INSPIRATION" MORE THAN MERE "PROVIDENCE"

The answer is, Nothing is needed beyond mere providence to secure such books — provided only that it does not lie in the Divine purpose that these books should possess qualities which rise above the powers of men to produce, even under the most complete Divine guidance. For providence is guidance; and guidance can bring one only so far as his own power can carry him. If heights are to be scaled above man's native power to achieve, then something more than guidance, however effective, is necessary. This is the reason for the superinduction, at the end of the long process of the production of Scripture, of the additional Divine operation which we call technically "inspiration." By it, the Spirit of God, flowing confluently in with the providentially and graciously determined work of men, spontaneously producing under the Divine directions the writings appointed to them, gives the product a Divine quality unattainable by human powers alone. Thus, these books become not merely the word of godly men, but the immediate word of God Himself, speaking directly as such to the minds and hearts of every reader. The value of "inspiration" emerges, thus, as twofold. It gives to the books written under its "bearing" a quality which is truly superhuman; a trustworthiness, an authority, a searchingness, a profundity, a profitableness which is altogether Divine. And it speaks this Divine word immediately to each reader's heart and conscience; so that he does not require to make his way to God, painfully, perhaps even uncertainly, through the words of His servants, the human instruments in writing the Scriptures, but can listen directly to the Divine voice itself speaking immediately in the Scriptural word to him.

WITNESS OF NEW TESTAMENT WRITERS TO DIVINE OPERATION

That the writers of the New Testament themselves conceive the Scriptures to have been produced thus by Divine operations extending through the increasing ages and involving a multitude of varied activities, can be made clear by simply attending to the occasional references they make to this or that step in the process. It lies, for example, on the face of their expositions, that they looked upon the Biblical history as teleological. Not only do they tell us that to "whatsoever things were written afore-time were written for our learning, that through patience and through comfort of the scriptures we might have hope" (Rom 15:4; compare Rom 4:23, 14); they speak also of the course of the historical events themselves as guided for our benefit: "Now these things happened unto them by way of example" — in a typical fashion, in such a way that, as they occurred, a typical character, or predictive reference impressed itself upon them; that is to say, briefly, the history occurred as it did in order to bear a message to us — "and they were written for our admonition, upon whom the ends of the ages are come" (1 Cor 10:11; compare 10:6). Accordingly, it has become a commonplace of Biblical exposition that "the history of redemption itself is a typically progressive one" (Küper), and is "in a manner impregnated with the prophetic element," so as to form a "part of a great plan which stretches from the fall of man to the first consummation of all things in glory; and, in so far as it reveals the mind of God toward man, carries a respect to the future not less than to the present" (P. Fairbairn). It lies equally on the face of the New Testament allusions to the subject that its writers understood that the preparation of men to become vehicles of God's message to man was not of yesterday, but had its beginnings in the very origin of their being. The call by which Paul, for example, was made an apostle of Jesus Christ was sudden and apparently without antecedents; but it is precisely this Paul who reckons this call as only one step in a long process, the beginnings of which antedated his own existence: "But when it was the good pleasure of God, who separated me, even from my mother's womb, and called me through his grace, to reveal his Son in me" (Gal 1:15, 16; compare Jer 1:5; Isa 49:1, 5). The recognition by the writers of the New Testament of the experiences of God's grace, which had been vouchsafed to them as an integral element in their fitting to be the bearers of His gospel to others, finds such pervasive expression that the only difficulty is to select from the mass the most illustrative passages. Such a statement as Paul gives in the opening verses of 2 Cor is thoroughly typical. There he represents that he has been afflicted and comforted to the end that he might "be able to comfort them that are in any affliction, through the comfort wherewith" he had himself been "comforted of God." For, he explains, "Whether we are afflicted, it is for your comfort and salvation; or whether we are comforted, it is for your comfort, which worketh in the patient enduring of the same sufferings which we also suffer" (2 Cor 1:4-6). It is beyond question, therefore, that the New Testament writers, when they declare the Scriptures to be the product of the Divine breath, and explain this as meaning that the writers of these Scriptures wrote them only as borne by the Holy Spirit in such a fashion that they spoke, not out of themselves, but "from God," are thinking of this operation of the Spirit only as the final act of God in the production of the Scriptures, superinduced upon a long series of processes, providential, gracious, miraculous, by which the matter of Scripture had been prepared for writing, and the men for writing it, and the writing of it had been actually brought to pass. It is this final act in the production of Scripture which is technically called "inspiration"; and inspiration is thus brought before us as, in the minds of the writers of the New Testament, that particular operation of God in the production of Scripture which takes effect at the very point of the writing of Scripture — understanding the term "writing" here as inclusive of all the processes of the actual composition of Scripture, the investigation of documents, the collection of facts, the excogitation of conclusions, the adaptation of exhortations as means to ends and the like — with the effect of giving to the resultant Scripture a specifically supernatural character, and constituting it a Divine, as well as human, book. Obviously the mode of operation of this Divine activity moving to this result is conceived, in full accord with the analogy of the Divine operations in other spheres of its activity, in providence and in grace alike, as confluent with the human activities operative in the case; as, in

i.e. the consideration of conclusions

a word, of the nature of what has come to be known as "immanent action."

"INSPIRATION" AND "REVELATION"

It will not escape observation that thus "inspiration" is made a mode of "revelation." We are often exhorted, to be sure, to distinguish sharply between "inspiration" and "revelation"; and the exhortation is just when "revelation" is taken in one of its narrower senses, of, say, an external manifestation of God, or of an immediate communication from God in words. But "inspiration" does not differ from "revelation" in these narrowed senses as genus from genus, but as a species of one genus differs from another. That operation of God which we call "inspiration," that is to say, that operation of the Spirit of God by which He "bears" men in the process of composing Scripture, so that they write, not of themselves, but "from God," is one of the modes in which God makes known to men His being, His will, His operations, His purposes. It is as distinctly a mode of revelation as any mode of revelation can be, and therefore it performs the same office which all revelation performs, that is to say, in the express words of Paul, it makes men wise, and makes them wise unto salvation. All "special" or "supernatural" revelation (which is redemptive in its very idea, and occupies a place as a substantial element in God's redemptive processes) has precisely this for its end; and Scripture, as a mode of the redemptive revelation of God, finds its fundamental purpose just in this: if the "inspiration" by which Scripture is produced renders it trustworthy and authoritative, it renders it trustworthy and authoritative only that it may the better serve to make men wise unto salvation. Scripture is conceived, from the point of view of the writers of the New Testament, not merely as the record of revelations, but as itself a part of the redemptive revelation of God; not merely as the record of the redemptive acts by which God is saving the world, but as itself one of these redemptive acts, having its own part to play in the great work of establishing and building up the kingdom of God. What gives it a place among the redemptive acts of God is its Divine origination, taken in its widest sense, as inclusive of all the Divine operations, providential, gracious and expressly supernatural, by which it has been made just what it is — a body of writings able to make wise unto salvation, and profitable for making the man of God perfect. What gives it its place among the modes of revelation is, however, specifically the culminating one of these Divine operations, which

Warfield's point here is that we must understand inspiration as a subset of the doctrine of God, specifically, of divine revelation. God has revealed himself, made himself known, in various ways. But Scripture is understood as the climax of divine revelation, for it is his very word. Scripture is God speaking.

Note here again that because Scripture is God's word, it cannot be rightly described as a mere "record" of divine revelation. Scripture, being God's word, IS divine revelation – it is God speaking, God making himself known to us.

we call "inspiration"; that is to say, the action of the Spirit of God in so "bearing" its human authors in their work of producing Scripture, as that in these Scriptures they speak, not out of themselves, but "from God." It is this act by virtue of which the Scriptures may properly be called "God-breathed."

SCRIPTURES A DIVINE-HUMAN BOOK?

It has been customary among a certain school of writers to speak of the Scriptures, because thus "inspired," as a Divine-human book, and to appeal to the analogy of Our Lord's Divine-human personality to explain their peculiar qualities as such. The expression calls attention to an important fact, and the analogy holds good a certain distance. There are human and Divine sides to Scripture, and, as we cursorily examine it, we may perceive in it, alternately, traits which suggest now the one, now the other factor in its origin. But the analogy with our Lord's Divine-human personality may easily be pressed beyond reason. There is no hypostatic union between the Divine and the human in Scripture; we cannot parallel the "inscripturation" of the Holy Spirit and the incarnation of the Son of God. The Scriptures are merely the product of Divine and human forces working together to produce a product in the production of which the human forces work under the initiation and prevalent direction of the Divine: the person of our Lord unites in itself Divine and human natures, each of which retains its distinctness while operating only in relation to the other. Between such diverse things there can exist only a remote analogy; and, in point of fact, the analogy in the present instance amounts to no more than that in both cases Divine and human factors are involved, though very differently. In the one they unite to constitute a Divine-human person, in the other they cooperate to perform a Divine-human work. Even so distant an analogy may enable us, however, to recognize that as, in the case of our Lord's person, the human nature remains truly human while yet it can never fall into sin or error because it can never act out of relation with the Divine nature into conjunction with which it has been brought; so in the case of the production of Scripture by the conjoint action of human and Divine factors, the human factors have acted as human factors and have left their mark on the product as such, and yet cannot have fallen into that error which we say it is human to fall into, because they have not acted apart from the Divine factors, by themselves, but only under their unerring guidance. P

Warfield's caution here has become important in our own day, for some have indeed pressed the analogy of Scripture and Christ's incarnation too far. The difference must be recognised: the Lord Jesus is himself fully human and fully divine; Scripture is a book that has come by means of God working through human beings. Our Lord is divine and human as to his natures and person; Scripture is divine and human as to its production.

This chapter is taken from *Confident: Why we can trust the Bible* by Michael Ovey and Daniel Strange, published by Christian Focus Publications, Fearn, Ross-shire, Scotland (www.christianfocus.com) and is used with their kind permission.

Reassuringly Unfashionable

One of the biggest challenges to taking the Bible seriously has to do with the perceived cultural offensiveness and irrelevance of the Bible to the enlightened twenty-first century mind. We all know the various hot-spots: sexuality, gender, genocide, slavery, science, judgment, hell, and so on. How do we deal with this perception?

First, we need to ask people, gently and respectfully, to tell us in more detail what specific problems they are talking about, and where they have come from. Then we just listen and see what happens. In our experience, many of these problems are not particularly well formed; in reality, there might be some simple factual things that we can clear up straightaway. Partly this might mean going back to the old issues of authority again. There is a real difference between 'I've got this real problem with issue x in the Bible. I've read it, re-read it, read around it, seen what the alternatives are...', and 'I saw this documentary on Channel 5 that said...' (or it might be, 'When we did R.E. at school, the teacher said...' or even 'My mate said...'). If a person has problems without ever having opened the Bible itself, isn't this a great opportunity for us to get it open with our friend together, even if we have to go away first and do a little preparation beforehand? Remember that people's doubts about the Bible, which we might think are so strong, are actually beliefs (albeit wrong) about the Bible which they have probably not thought about much and so have taken on faith, which is probably pretty fuzzy-sighted.

Second, we need to get people thinking a little bit about culture and our place in history. Here's an illustration that's been useful in trying to chip away at this negative perception and turn it into a positive. One reason to pick up the Bible and have a look is that it is 'reassuringly unfashionable':

> In the late 80s, the infamous 'Tots' nightclub in Southend-on-Sea had a fancy dress competition every year on Boxing Day. I was desperate to win and so raided my dad's wardrobe for a suitable costume.
>
> Now my dad was from Guyana in South America and had come over to the U.K. in the late 60s, married my mum and had yours truly. At that time they were a striking couple. My dad was a handsome chap and his clothes and hair in the 70s made him look very similar to Shaft (google it!), complete with Afro and amazing sideburns.
>
> So just think of the sartorial treasures I uncovered for the fancy dress party – various patterned silk shirts, cravats, medallions (yes, medallions!), bell bottom suede brown flares, etc. Everyone, including me, thought I looked absolutely ridiculous, outrageous, offensive. I was a walking fashion crime against humanity. I won £10. (Worth a bit back then).
>
> Here's the thing: I know that in the next year or so, my eldest son is going to come to me and say, 'Dad, I've got this fancy dress party coming up, can I have a look in your wardrobe for some clothes crimes, please?'

You see, we still tend to think that our particular stage in the history of humanity is the most enlightened and liberative, that we have a perspective not bound by cultural blind-spots and prejudices. Basically we think that we are 'it'. But we know that in the not-too-distant future, people will look back and think we were so outdated. We do it now. One of us confesses:

> I celebrated my twenty-year wedding anniversary a few months ago. Looking through our wedding day photos, at one point I just turned to my wife and said a little crossly, 'Were you playing a practical joke on me in 1994? Why on earth did you allow me to wear those glasses which covered my whole face' – three years before Harry Potter! – 'and that wavy haircut?' But of course, I thought back then I was making the ultimate attempt to look good, and just so she doesn't get out of it, I must say that I think my wife thought I looked good too!

The bottom line is this: are we going to ditch the Bible and its amazing good news for humanity with its eternal implications, just because there is a cultural issue we have now that we know may not be an issue in seventy-five years' time?

We can say a bit more on this. In his little book *Persuasions*, which is an apologetic *Pilgrim's Progress*, Doug Wilson deals with this issue of the Bible and culture, as the main character, Evangelist, encounters the Rev. Daniel Howe, who questions that the Bible is God's Word. Daniel says to Evangelist:

Doug Wilson, *Persuasions* (Moscow, ID: Canon Press, 1989), 38.

'It sounds very pious to speak of "God's Word", but you neglect the work of very serious biblical scholars. Modern scholarship indicates that those who wrote the Bible were products of their culture. They wrote as fallible men.'

'You seem to indicate that you think it is not good to be a product of your culture.'

'Why, certainly. If someone writes within the framework of a particular culture, they cannot see it with objectivity.'

'And do modern scholars write from within a culture or not?'

Daniel stopped. 'What do you mean?'

'You don't trust the apostle Paul because he wrote within the first century. Why don't you mistrust modern scholars for the same reason? They write within the twentieth.'

'But modern scholars have good reasons for saying the things they do. They are able to reason objectively.'

'So then, you believe it is possible for a writer to transcend the culture he grew up in?'

'Well, yes.'

'I'm glad to hear you say that. That is what the biblical writers did.'

Daniel appeared to be at a loss for words.

Evangelist continued. 'We know that the biblical writers were willing to challenge their culture with the Word of God, whenever they saw that such a rebuke was needed. They prophesied and spoke against their contemporaries time and again – far more than modern scholars do. If anyone in history was free of contemporary prejudices they were.'

Because the Bible is what it says it is, not simply a product of culture but a word from another world, although we are earth bound and culture bound, the Bible isn't. We don't sit in judgment over it; it sits in judgment over us.

Finally, we can turn a perceived negative into a positive. In one of his best-ever illustrations Tim Keller asks whether we really want a god who functions as a robot (like the wives do in the film, *The Stepford Wives*), who does everything we say and do, and agrees with everything we say and do. Sure, it might be fun for a while, but this isn't really the stuff of intimate personal relationships which are real ones:

> *Now what happens if you eliminate anything from the Bible that offends your sensibility and crosses your will? If you pick and choose what you want to believe and reject the rest, how will you ever have a God who can contradict you? You won't! You'll have a Stepford God. A God, essentially, of your own making, and not a God with whom you can have a relationship and genuine interaction. Only if your God can say things that can outrage you and make you struggle (as in a real friendship or marriage) will you know that you have got hold of a real God and not a figment of your imagination. So an authoritative Bible is not the enemy of a personal relationship with God. It is a precondition for it.*

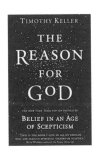

Tim Keller, *The Reason for God* (London: Hodder, 2008), 114.

THE GOD BEHIND THE GENOCIDE

How should we understand the conquest of Canaan?

by Dave Puttick

The God of the Old Testament is arguably the most unpleasant character in all fiction: jealous and proud of it; a petty, unjust, unforgiving control-freak; a vindictive, bloodthirsty ethnic cleanser; a misogynistic, homophobic, racist, infanticidal, genocidal, filicidal, pestilential, megalomaniac, sadomasochistic, capriciously malevolent bully.

Richard Dawkins, *The God Delusion* (London: Bantam, 2006), 31.

So writes Richard Dawkins in his bestselling tract against religion, *The God Delusion*. It's easy to dismiss this as mere rhetorical showmanship, but Dawkins and the so-called 'New Atheists' raise important questions that resonate both in our culture and our churches. For many readers of Scripture, both Christian and non-Christian, the conquest narratives of Joshua are the place where they feel most keenly Dawkins' charges of genocide and ethnic cleansing. What are we to make of the report that Joshua and his men "devoted the city to the LORD and destroyed with the sword every living thing in it – men and women, young and old" (Josh 6:21)? More than that, what are we to make of the explicit sanction of such activity by Yahweh? Is Dawkins right about God after all? Do these stories present insurmountable problems for evangelical Christians?

Some have concluded so. In his recent book *The Bible Tells Me So*, Peter Enns argues that the treatment of the Canaanites is indefensible, and we need to stop trying to defend it. Unlike the New Atheists, Enns

wants to hold on to the belief that God is there, and is loving. But, like the New Atheists, Enns views the Old Testament (OT) narratives, at least in this instance, as fictional. He argues that God didn't command those things and even that they didn't really happen. Instead he puts it all down the ancient Israelites crafting stories of their past to make sense of the present, speaking in "their cultural language" about God, or rather, how they *"experienced God."* Indeed he thinks that's the only possible answer. To preserve our belief in God's goodness he insists we need to find ways to distance God from the ways he is spoken about in the Bible.

But is it possible to uphold God's goodness *and* the Bible's reliability even in this passage of Scripture? Yes! And we will be able to see that when we understand the conquest narratives within their contexts: the OT as a whole, salvation history and, ultimately, the nature of a holy God as he has revealed himself. As each of these contexts is considered in turn, a clearer picture will emerge.

ibid., 63.

ibid., 65, emphasis original.

Peter Enns, *The Bible Tells Me So: Why Defending Scripture Has Made Us Unable to Read It* (San Francisco: HarperOne, 2014), 58.

Filling out the picture: *God and war in the Old Testament*

F. Derek Kidner, "Old Testament Perspectives on War." *The Evangelical Quarterly* 57.2 (April-June 1985), 100.

Joshua must first be understood as only a part, rather than the totality, of what the OT says about Yahweh, his people, and warfare. Derek Kidner distinguishes three types of war in the OT: wars of aggression, wars of defence or liberation, and wars of divine judgement. Joshua presents wars of the third kind, but this is by no means the usual pattern of warfare in the OT. In the laws for war in Deuteronomy 20, there is a sharp distinction between the way wars are to be conducted in the normal course of things, and the way in which the conquest is to take place. The "devotion to destruction" of the cities of the Canaanites, detailed in 20:16-18 (do not leave alive anything that breathes – 20:16), contrasts with the situation regarding "cities that are at a distance from you" in 20:10-15 ("make its people an offer of peace" – 20:10). As David Howard writes in his commentary on Joshua, "the instructions to Israel to annihilate the Canaanites were specific in time, intent, and geography ... Israel was not given a blanket permission to do the same to any peoples they encountered, at any time or in any place."

David M. Howard Jr., *Joshua* (NAC 5; Nashville: Broadman & Holman, 1998), 186.

Indeed 1 Kings 20:31 indicates that Israel and her kings later earned a reputation amongst the surrounding nations for mercy, not savagery:

1 Kings 20:31 | *[Ben-Hadad, king of Syria's] officials said to him, "Look, we have heard that the kings of Israel are merciful. Let us go to the king of Israel with sackcloth around our waists and ropes around our heads. Perhaps he will spare your life."*

Chris Wright's assessment of Dawkins is apposite:

> *It is a caricature of the Old Testament to portray God as constantly on the warpath or to portray the conquest as simply 'typical' of the rest of the story. It is not.*

Christopher J. H. Wright, *The God I Don't Understand* (Grand Rapids: Zondervan, 2008), 90.

Enns, *The Bible Tells Me So*, 46, emphasis original.

It should be noted at this point what we are *not* saying. Enns accuses traditional biblical interpreters of "trying to get God off the hook" by saying *"Sure, God killed the Canaanites, but we have to balance it out with those parts where God was nicer."* It is not a question of balance, nor are we seeking to avoid the issue by pointing to more comfortable portraits of God in the OT. We simply plead for the total witness of Scripture to be taken into account, rather than one (misunderstood) part being magnified to caricature.

That said, the conquest narratives are part of that total witness, even if they are only a small part. To understand them we need to place Joshua in the context of salvation history. Before we tackle that, it will be worth pausing to defend the historicity of the Bible's account of the conquest of Canaan.

Much ado about nothing: *Did the conquest ever take place?*

Enns is sceptical of the Bible's record of events:

Biblical archaeologists are about as certain as you can be about these things that the conquest of Canaan as the Bible describes it did not happen: no mass invasion from the outside by an Israelite army, and no extermination of Canaanites as God commanded.

Enns, *The Bible Tells Me So*, 58.

Such claims should in turn be treated with a degree of scepticism. Much of the Ancient Near East (ANE) remains to be excavated, and as even Enns admits, archaeologists are "not always right, they disagree with each other, they can have blind spots like the rest of us mortals." Nonetheless, we must consider what the best available evidence suggests.

ibid., 58.

K.A. Kitchen, *On the Reliability of the Old Testament* (Grand Rapids: Eerdmans, 2003), 160-161, Table 8.

We begin though with the biblical text itself. Kenneth Kitchen, in his monumental *On the Reliability of the Old Testament*, notes that throughout Joshua 1-14, there is no full-scale occupation of the land over the dead bodies of the Canaanites. Rather, Israel camps at Gilgal and repeatedly returns there from raids upon the major centres (Jericho, Ai, and Hazor – Josh 11:13 speaks of other cities that "Israel did not burn"). In the later chapters of Joshua, we begin to see occupation of the land, but even at the end of the book Joshua speaks to the leaders of Israel concerning the danger of "these nations that remain among you" (Josh 23:12), and the conquest remains incomplete in Judges 1. The biblical text, when carefully examined, suggests that we should not be looking for archaeological evidence of instant and total conquest. As Kitchen puts it:

ibid., 163.

> *Insofar as only Jericho, Ai, and Hazor were explicitly allowed to have been burned into nonoccupation, it is also pointless going looking for extensive conflagration levels at any other Late Bronze sites (of any phase) to identify them with any Israelite impact.*

In other words, sceptical archaeologists are seeking something that the biblical text itself does not encourage them to seek.

What the biblical text *does* lead us to expect is exactly what we know of the ANE context:

ibid., 165.

1) displaced people groups seeking to raid cities and establish themselves in certain locations,

Kitchen locates the Biblical town of Adam at present-day Tell ed-Damieh: "It is specifically in this district that the high banks of the Jordan have been liable to periodic collapses, sufficient to block the river for a time." He gives examples of this in A.D. 1267, 1906 and 1927. *ibid.*, 167.

2) periodic collapses in the high banks of the Jordan leading to the stopping of the waters, just as in Josh 3:16,

ibid., 175-176.

3) plausible names of people and groups current in the second millennium B.C.

Moreover, for at least one of the towns destroyed in the Joshua account, Hazor, there is considerable evidence for its destruction in a conflagration in the late thirteenth century B.C., which fits well with the biblical data. *ibid.*, 185. Thus, if we read the biblical text carefully and consider the ANE background soberly, we see that the two cohere. Salvation history is *historical reality*.

Devoted to destruction: *The salvation-historical purposes of the 'ḥerem'*

We return now to the central question: what is the place of the conquest narratives within salvation history? In other words, why did Yahweh command this specific instance of the total destruction of the cities of Canaan? The OT's answer is twofold: for the sanctification of Israel and its land to Yahweh, and as a punishment for the heinous sins of the Canaanites. As we come to the NT, we see a third reason: to lead us to Christ.

To sanctify Israel

The language of sanctification points to the religious context of the command to "destroy totally" the inhabitants of Canaan. The Hebrew word used in commands such as those in Deuteronomy 7:2 and 20:17, which frame the Joshua narratives, is *ḥerem*. This word occurs in a religious context in the laws about vows in Leviticus 27:20-29. J.P.U. Lilley notes that, "a distinction is made between dedicating (*haqdîš*) and devoting (*haḥᵃrîm*); that which is dedicated can be redeemed, that which is devoted cannot." Similarly in Exodus 22:20, Yahweh "decrees this fate for an apostate and uses the *ḥerem* terminology." The root idea is one of "irrevocable renunciation of any interest in the object 'devoted'." When carried over into a military context in Deuteronomy 7, the *ḥerem* means not only slaughtering the inhabitants of the land (7:2a), but avoiding any kind of covenant with them (7:2b), avoiding intermarriage with them (7:3) and breaking down their idols (7:5). The emphasis is on the total separation of the Israelites from the idolatry of the pagan nations.

Why this emphasis? The answer is plain in the Deuteronomy passages. In 7:4, intermarriage poses the danger that, "they will turn your children away from following me to serve other gods." Again, in 20:18 *ḥerem* is decreed "otherwise, they will teach you to follow all the detestable things they do in worshiping their gods, and you will sin against the LORD your God." Within the larger context of the covenant, it is about preserving the holiness of God's chosen people.

Within an even wider frame, this holiness of Israel is for the good of the world, as Israel was to function as "a kingdom of priests and a holy nation" among the peoples of the earth (Exod 19:6), to demonstrate the wisdom of God to the world by their obedience to God's law (Deut 4:6-8).

The establishment of Israel in the land served, for a limited time, to further God's covenant purpose of blessing the nations.

J.P.U. Lilley, "Understanding the Herem." *Tyndale Bulletin* 44.1 (1993), 173.

Kidner, "Old Testament Perspectives on War," 103.

Lilley, "Understanding the *Herem*," 176.

See Deut 7:6, echoing the language of the covenant initiation in Exod 19:5-6.

Paul Copan, *Is God a Moral Monster? Making Sense of the Old Testament God* (Grand Rapids: Baker, 2011), 191.

As the Israelites stood on the brink of entering the land that Yahweh had promised on oath to Abraham, that same land was full of idolatrous practices, practices that the Israelites had already shown themselves all too willing to become entangled in – worshipping the Baal of Peor in Numbers 25, for example. The ḥerem served as a kind of protection against such entrapment. It may seem a stark kind of protection to the 21st century reader but, as Philip Jenson puts it, it seems to have been "the only realistic possibility of creating a society and culture that held fast to the true God ... The need for such stark laws is a witness to the tendency for human beings to prefer idols to the living God." Far from revealing God as a moral monster, the Canaanite episode serves as a poignant witness to humanity's monstrous, immoral tendency to worship things that are not God, to overturn the distinction between Creator and creatures, and to rebel against our rightful king.

Philip Jenson, *The Problem of War in the Old Testament* (Grove Biblical Series 25; Cambridge: Grove, 2002), 14.

It is worth pausing to consider why we find this so hard to accept. To quote Jenson again, "The seriousness of this instruction is ... a corollary of the deadly seriousness of avoiding idolatry, the first commandment." That first commandment, like all of the commandments, derives its seriousness from the God who gives it:

ibid., 14.

> *Deut 5:6*　　"I am the LORD your God, who brought you out of Egypt, out of the land of slavery."

Perhaps our horror at the Biblical notion of ḥerem derives ultimately from a truncated view of Yahweh's unique holiness. That is to say, questions about OT ethics are, in the final analysis, questions about OT theology.

The question of who God is must precede all other questions. The discomfort for us is that confronting the true God means seeing ourselves in all the ugliness of our depravity. Human pride and self-deception about the depths of that depravity quickly becomes a barrier to reading the Bible sensitively and doing theology responsibly.

To punish the Canaanites

At the same time, some of our distaste for the ḥerem comes because we wrongly think of it in terms of ethnic cleansing. Wright reminds us, "the conquest of Canaan is *never* justified on ethnic grounds in the Bible." The salvation of Rahab and her family indicates this, as does the presence of "foreigners" among the people of Israel in Josh 8:35. Indeed, the Mosaic Law enshrined the protection of strangers and aliens within Israel (e.g. Lev 19:34; Deut 10:18-19), so it can hardly be right to caricature Yahweh as a bloodthirsty xenophobe.

Rather, alongside the idea of sanctifying Israel and the land to Yahweh, the proper context for understanding the conquest narratives is one of punishment for sin. This can be seen in the rationale given in Deut 9:5:

Wright, *The God I Don't Understand*, 92, emphasis original.

Copan, *Is God a Moral Monster?*, 178, points out that Rahab's salvation further indicates that the ḥerem was not "absolute and irreversible."

See Copan, *Moral Monster*, 163-165.

> *Deut 9:5*
>
> **It is not because of your righteousness or your integrity that you are going in to take possession of their land; but on account of the wickedness of these nations, the LORD your God will drive them out before you, to accomplish what he swore to your fathers, to Abraham, Isaac and Jacob.**

This builds on Gen 15:16, where Abraham is told that his descendants will return to Canaan "In the fourth generation... for the sin of the Amorites has not yet reached its full measure." Yahweh exercises patience in not destroying the Amorites (Canaanites) at first, but in giving them time to "complete" their iniquity. Enns suggests that Gen 15:16 is a case of God "giving the Canaanites enough rope with which to hang themselves," rather than any kind of grace. But this ignores the reality that the patriarchs were living amongst these peoples, acting as a blessing to the nations, if the nations would "bless" them (Gen 12:1-3). When destruction finally does come, the news of the coming Israelite army has preceded them (Josh 2:9-11), offering a chance for Canaanites like Rahab to repent and join the people of God. As Paul Copan puts it, "Just as a pagan Nineveh repented at the sight and message of ... Jonah, the Canaanites could have repented – unless, of course, they were too far gone morally and spiritually."

Enns, *The Bible Tells Me So*, 35.

Copan, *Is God a Moral Monster?*, 178.

The witness of Scripture is that the Canaanites *were* "too far gone", and were destroyed because of their wickedness. This may not be unproblematic for the modern reader, but nonetheless,

" *The use of violence within a framework of justice and punishment ... is not simply indistinguishable from the use of violence in wantonly selfish, arbitrary, and malevolent ways.*

Wright, *The God I Don't Understand*, 94.

Offering a child sacrifice to the idol Molech, as featured in Charles Foster, *Bible Pictures and What They Teach Us*, (Philadelphia: W. A. Foster, 1897), p74.

This theme of the punishment of the Canaanites' sin is seen starkly in Leviticus 18. As Yahweh outlaws all kinds of sexual perversions, he draws a distinction between his people and the Canaanites: "you must not do as they do in the land of Canaan, where I am bringing you" (Lev 18:3). Why? Because "the nations that I am going to drive out before you became defiled. Even the land was defiled; so I punished it for its sin, and the land vomited out its inhabitants" (Lev 18:24-25). The list of practices to which Yahweh is referring includes incest (18:6), child sacrifice (18:21), and bestiality (18:23). Howard puts it well: "By the standards of most cultures, the sins of Leviticus 18:6-23 are particularly heinous." The God of the OT is not indifferent to such sins.

Howard, *Joshua*, 185.

Nor is he partial, treating his people with one standard and the nations with another. Copan observes that in Deut 13:12-18 the same sanction of ḥerem is decreed against Israelite cities that go over to idolatry as to Canaanite cities. Further, whilst in the conquest God's holiness meant that he destroyed the nations at the hands of Israel, later he used the nations to destroy Israel for her idolatry (1 Kgs 17:6-20). In both cases Yahweh is vindicated as a holy and truth-speaking Lord.

Pitkänen suggests that "the appeal to [the Canaanites'] sinfulness can be seen as part of a standard strategy of demonization and dehumanization of the opposition ... in order to rationalize acts of violence." But this fails to take into account the honesty of the Pentateuch about the Israelites' own sinful behaviour. Pekka M. Pitkänen, *Joshua* (Apollos Old Testament Commentary 6; Nottingham: Apollos, 2010), 79.

Copan, *Is God a Moral Monster?*, 163.

Once again, getting the holiness of God and the sinfulness of sin right precedes a right understanding of the ethics of the conquest. These, then, are the contexts for the conquest stories within the OT's grand story: the sanctification of Israel and its land to Yahweh and the punishment of the heinous sins of the Canaanites. In short, *"The conquest was not human genocide. It was divine judgement."*

Wright, *The God I Don't Understand*, 93.

To lead us to Christ

The situation of the Israelites does not map neatly onto our present situation as Christians within pluralistic states, because it is illegitimate to identify God's people under the new covenant with any nation state, as Don Carson observes:

D.A. Carson, *How Long, O Lord? Reflections on Suffering and Evil* (2d ed.; Nottingham: IVP, 2006), 86.

One of the fundamental differences brought about by the new covenant is the fact that the locus of the people of God under this covenant no longer constitutes a nation, but an international community not to be identified with any nation.

Further:

Every attempt to establish a unified "Christian nation," where the respective boundaries of church and state are made to coalesce, has not only been misconceived but has resulted in disastrous failure.

ibid., 89.

Clearing away this misconception – that present nations can somehow enforce the boundaries of God's kingdom – helps to undercut the force of Enns's critique that "Christians, taking the Bible as a how-to book, have killed pagans, taken their land, and rejoiced in God's goodness." Even in the OT, the kind of "holy war" seen in Joshua was not to take place without explicit special revelation. The problem is not the OT, but the misapplication of the OT.

Enns, *The Bible Tells Me So*, 30.

Copan, *Is God a Moral Monster?*, 161.

Yet the God of the OT *is* the God of the New. Christians cannot adopt any variety of the Marcionite heresy when it comes to uncomfortable passages in the OT. Yahweh is our God, and it is not as if his holiness or standards for judgement have changed. Rather, in the NT, "the historical, earthly judgements of God in the Old Testament are used as case studies and warnings in relation to the even worse judgement to come."

Marcion was a second century heretic who argued the law-giving Creator of the OT was different to the gracious God revealed in the person of Jesus. As a result he largely rejected the OT and heavily edited the NT gospels and letters, removing references to the OT.

Wright, *The God I Don't Understand*, 81. Tellingly, Enns's handling of the teaching of Jesus and the doctrine of hell is weak: "What Jesus means by 'hell' isn't worse than what God did to the Canaanites." – Enns, *The Bible Tells Me So*, 43.

Ultimately too, the cross is the place where those two themes – the purity of God's people and the judgment of sin - come together, God's sinful people's sins are cleansed and their judgment is borne by God himself in the person of his Son.

The conquest narratives, as the rest of the OT, were "written down as warnings for us, on whom the culmination of the ages has come" (1 Cor 10:11). Their ultimate purpose was to lead us to Christ, who is, as it were, "devoted to complete destruction," subjected to ḥerem in place of undeserving sinners like us.

In conclusion: *Reading Scripture and encountering the holy God*

We must acknowledge the difficulty of finding an answer to the 'problem' of the Canaanite episode that will satisfy the non-Christian reader of Scripture. The conquest narratives presuppose the wickedness of idolatry: wickedness so grave that Yahweh must punish it with total destruction, whilst also preserving his chosen people from the danger of entanglement in it. Even to hint at such an idea leads to "a serious questioning of modern values," as Jenson notes. Our sense of moral outrage at acts motivated by the holiness of God is, as Carson puts it, "one more indication that we have given ourselves to thinking great thoughts about human beings and small thoughts about God." Understanding the conquest aright will involve significant revision of those habits of thought.

Jenson, *The Problem of War*, 14.

Carson, *How Long O Lord?*, 86.

The challenge for the Christian reader is to extract ourselves from those ways of thinking shaped by our postmodern culture and try to think God's thoughts after him. We should not start from the 'problem', but from a robust doctrine of God's holiness and goodness. In that light we will learn to deal with things that we still find mysterious about God, and to recognise our own complicity in the sin that deserves death. That process of reflection ought, ultimately, to lead not to "arrogant self-righteousness and shocked, condescending horror, but contrition, brokenness, intercession," for we can only begin to understand the conquest of Canaan from the foot of the cross. P

Carson, *How Long O Lord?*, 90.

Further reading

Helpful chapters in three books responding to the apologetic issues raised by the conquest of Canaan, as well as a host of other 'moral problems' in the OT, and the bigger question of suffering and evil in the Bible:

Carson, D.A. *How Long, O Lord? Reflections on Suffering and Evil.* 2d. ed. (Nottingham: IVP, 2006), 83-96.
Copan, Paul, *Is God a Moral Monster? Making Sense of the Old Testament God* (Grand Rapids: Baker, 2011) 156-197.
Wright, Christopher J.H., *The God I Don't Understand* (Grand Rapids: Zondervan, 2008) 76-110.

Some shorter and more technical articles:

Jenson, Philip, *The Problem of War in the Old Testament,* Grove Biblical Series 25 (Cambridge: Grove, 2002).
Kidner, F. Derek, "Old Testament Perspectives on War." *The Evangelical Quarterly* 57.2 (April-June 1985), 99-113.
Lilley, J.P.U., "Understanding the Herem," *Tyndale Bulletin 44.1* (1993), 169-177.

For help on the issues of archaeology and biblical history, this is the 'gold standard' conservative work – but be warned, it's a dense read:

Kitchen, K.A. *On the Reliability of the Old Testament* (Grand Rapids: Eerdmans, 2003) 159-239 deals with the period before the kingdoms of David and Solomon.

As we think about how to defend and celebrate the gift of God's Word, we thought it would be great to sit down with a pastor and hear how his church has been defending the lion and enjoying its roar.

Ralph Cunnington is one of the pastors of City Church Manchester, a church which began in September 2014. Find out more about the church at *citychurchmanchester.org*

Acts 20:27 - "For I [Paul] have not hesitated to proclaim to you the whole will of God."

PRIMER: As you've planned your teaching programme at City Church Manchester, what's shaped the content?

RALPH: We have four key values at City Church: *Bible, Grace, Community* and *Engagement*. These values are so important to us that we spent the seven Sundays leading up to our launch preaching through an expository series on our aims and values as a church. The *Bible* value states: *"Bible – God's word transforms lives and therefore the Bible is foundational to all we do."* It's easy to say that, and indeed most churches claim that the Bible is foundational, but what does it look like in practice? For us it means a regular diet of sequential expository preaching: preaching consecutively through a book of the Bible, letting the main message of the passage be the main message of the sermon.

So far we have preached through Ephesians, Haggai, Genesis 1-11 and John 1-3. We think that the main diet of the church should be sequential expository preaching in both the Old and New Testaments (and combining a variety of genres) because we want God to set the agenda for our church. If Matt (my co-pastor) and I simply chose the passage (or topic) each week, we'd limit the church to our own Bible knowledge and ideas. By challenging ourselves to preach through whole books sequentially we are doing Acts 20:27 and ensuring that both we and the church are challenged and led in unexpected ways each week.

It is possible, however, to do expository teaching as part of a thematic series and this is what we chose to do in our midweek meetings for the first six months of the church. These meetings, called *Connect 4 Manchester*, try to combine the best parts of a midweek central church meeting (bringing together everyone, direct input from the pastors) with the intimacy and group learning dynamics of small groups. We meet at 7pm in the church building for food, followed by a 10-15 minute talk and one hour of Bible study and prayer in small groups.

Foundational

In the autumn term, we based our series around Tim Keller's *Gospel in Life*. City Church meets in the city centre of Manchester – a liberal and very much post-Christian city with thriving business and creative sectors. Too often, people (whether Christian or not) assume that Christianity is only relevant to their "spiritual lives" and hermetically seal off the rest of their lives. By opening the church with this midweek series we wanted to show that no such divide exists and to train our people to see how the gospel impacts and transforms every aspect of their lives. In short, we wanted to begin the church by living out our fourth value: *"Engagement – The gospel is great news for a lost world and therefore we are committed to applying it to every aspect of city life."*

Timothy Keller, *Gospel in Life* (Grand Rapids: Zondervan, 2010). Eight video sessions available on DVD or to download. Separate *Participant's Guide* also available.

PRIMER: You recently ran a short series on the doctrine of Scripture. Why that series in particular? What would you say to someone who said we don't need to defend scripture, or that debates about things like inerrancy aren't relevant in the UK?

RALPH: Because the Bible is foundational to the church (a truth stated in our values and of which we were reminded in our first series on Ephesians – Eph 2:20), we thought it was sensible to spend some time thinking about what exactly the Bible teaches about itself.

Eph 2:20 - Consequently, you are no longer foreigners and strangers, but fellow citizens with God's people and also members of his household, built on the foundation of the apostles and prophets, with Christ Jesus himself as the chief cornerstone.

We live in a culture where there is a general suspicion of truth claims and an almost total lack of biblical literacy. This impacts both Christians and unbelievers.

One of the things that struck us as we gathered the core team and met with people in Manchester from a Christian background, was how many of them had significant questions about what it meant for the Bible to be authoritative and true in everything it affirms. These are big and important questions and it was essential for us to address them very early in the life of the church.

to all we do.

The inerrancy debate in the US can sometimes come across as an unpleasant gate-keeping fight.

For us, inerrancy is a sweet and precious truth because it means that we can trust the sufficiency and authority of the Bible as we let it lead us through the good and the hard times as a church. Therefore it was crucial for us to be united in our commitment to it.

PRIMER: What exactly did the series look like?

Kevin DeYoung, *Taking God at His Word* (Nottingham: Inter-Varsity Press, 2014).

RALPH: We used Kevin DeYoung's short book, *Taking God at His Word*, as a rough guide for the series. We cut it down to six weeks and covered the key attributes of the Bible: *authority*, *inerrancy*, *sufficiency*, *necessity* and *clarity*. The series was titled *The Double-Edged Sword* and the intention with each session was to show how the particular attribute of Scripture was founded in the Bible itself and crucial to our day-to-day lives. We wanted our people to see that our doctrine of Scripture is immensely practical.

Each week began with a short talk from either Matt or myself which sought to engage people and help them to see the practical significance of the attribute that we were looking at. We would then break into small groups for a Bible study on a passage dealing with the particular attribute. Group leaders were provided with questions on the passage and a copy of DeYoung's book.

PRIMER: What are your reflections on how it went?

RALPH: It was great to see people growing in their delight in the Bible and their understanding of its significance to church life. For those who didn't understand the importance of the doctrines of inerrancy and sufficiency it was like a light going on which gave them greater confidence in the Bible. The series also provided an opportunity to look at and digest some of the historic Reformed confessions. The clarity of Scripture is often viewed as an obscure doctrine (ironically perpetuated by its classic label – *perspicuity*) but the Westminster Confession's statement in I.VII

I.VII - All things in Scripture are not alike plain in themselves, nor alike clear unto all: yet those things which are necessary to be known, believed, and observed for salvation are so clearly propounded, and opened in some place of Scripture or other, that not only the learned, but the unlearned, in a due use of the ordinary means, may attain unto a sufficient understanding of them.

proved immensely helpful to us in understanding what we should expect as we read the harder parts of Scripture. It was also wonderful for people to grasp the assurance that the sufficiency of Scripture gives to a new church plant.

We don't have a building, we only had 27 members, and we only have enough money in the bank to last three months, but in the Bible we have everything we need to be a display of God's glory in the centre of Manchester and beyond (Eph 3:8-10).

One of the by-products of the series was that people had a hunger to spend more time working through the Bible sequentially in small groups. The studies in the series were taken from different parts of the Bible and people sometimes struggled with understanding the context. We therefore decided that our next Connect series would be a 13-week series on Romans 1-8. We also realised that Connect group leaders needed more resources and training than the questions and DeYoung's book provided. We have since introduced hour-long Leader Training sessions at 6-7pm before Connect starts. These cover topics such as reading skills, group dynamics, preparing questions, pastoral care and other matters relating to leading small group Bible studies. The training sessions have been well received.

PRIMER: Which resources did you find most helpful in your own preparation and what did you find yourself recommending to others to read?

RALPH: DeYoung's book is a very helpful introduction and I would definitely recommend it to anyone as a first point of reference on the doctrine of Scripture. My favourite popular level book on the topic is Tim Ward's book, *Words of Life*. Like DeYoung's book, it looks at the attributes of Scripture but it does so using the tools of speech act theory. I think this is immensely helpful in showing what is going on whenever God speaks. It is thoroughly biblical (Isa 55:11) and fundamentally re-orientates what we should be expecting whenever we listen to the word preached or study it for ourselves. At a more advanced level, I have really enjoyed B.B. Warfield, *The Inspiration and Authority of the Bible*. P

Eph 3:8-10 - Although I am less than the least of all the Lord's people, this grace was given me: to preach to the Gentiles the boundless riches of Christ, and to make plain to everyone the administration of this mystery, which for ages past was kept hidden in God, who created all things. His intent was that now, through the church, the manifold wisdom of God should be made known to the rulers and authorities in the heavenly realms...

Isa 55:11
"...so is my word that goes out from my mouth: it will not return to me empty, but will accomplish what I desire and achieve the purpose for which I sent it."

THE CHURCH NEEDS MORE THEOLOGY AND THEOLOGY NEEDS MORE CHURCH

I recently read an article by Gerald Hiestand called

'A taxonomy of the Pastor-Theologian: Why PhD students should consider the pastorate as the context for their theological scholarship.'

Expository Times
124 (2013): 261–71.

Because he's writing in an American context and for PhD students (at least in the first instance) I may have lost you at "taxonomy," but I want to engage with this article as a roundabout way of introducing the ethos behind *Primer*. I'll outline the article first and then offer a number of reflections.

Outline

In a nutshell Hiestand thinks that the church needs more theology and that theology needs more church. He begins by noting that it has not always been this way. Throughout church history a great number of the leading figures have been pastor-theologians: Athanasius, Augustine, Luther, Calvin, Wesley and Edwards. More recently however, theology has taken a step away from the church as the *pastor-theologian* has been replaced by the *professor-theologian* – the full-time academic – and "this transition has not been without effect on the health of the Church or her theology, notably in two primary ways" (262):

1. "As the theologians moved from the pulpit to the lecture halls the theological water level within the pastoral community – and thus our congregations – fell considerably. The collective capacity of the pastoral community to think deeply and carefully about the crucial social, cultural and theological issues facing the church has waned. A vapid pragmatism has been the inevitable result" (262).

2. "Not only has the church become theologically anemic, but theology has become in many instances, ecclesially anemic," that is, it has been divorced from its true purpose, uprooted from its natural soil in the church and transplanted into academia. From as long ago as the twelfth century, theology has been relocated in the universities where theology is no longer serving the church or developing in response to its needs. Increasingly the modern university holds theologians to standards of objectivity and the "methodological agnosticism of the wider university is not without effect, even within the divinity schools. It does not take long to note the difference between the earnest, pastoral tone of a Calvin or Luther, and the more disinterested tone one often finds in a contemporary academic journal" (263).

Hiestand notes some progress in healing this divide but also some lingering problems. On the academic side he recognises that there are theologians with a concern for the local church but argues that it is "simply asking too much of academic theologians to be sufficiently aware of and driven by the questions of a social location [i.e. the church] that they do not vocationally inhabit" (264).

On the church side, Hiestand notes that pastor-theologians have some profile within the church but again he is concerned that contemporary conceptions of that role are inadequate to meet the need.

(264) To move forward we must assess the dominant understandings of the pastor-theologian with a view to articulating a fresh vision. From what I can observe, the term 'pastor-theologian' conveys two basic meanings: the pastor-theologian as *local theologian*, and the pastor theologian as *popular theologian*.

The *local theologian* is "the theologically astute pastor who ably services the theological needs of a local church, most immediately through a preaching ministry" but crucially his sense of theological responsibility "does not extend beyond one's own local congregation" (265). This pastor reads widely and fulfils the role David Wells outlines for the pastor-theologian in *No Place for Truth* – acting as a "'broker' of theological truth," an intermediary between professional theologians and the congregation.

The *popular theologian*, unlike the local theologian, is a writer. "Bridging the gap between the professional theological community and the local church, the popular theologian translates academic theology down to other pastors and the laity" (266). In addition the popular theologian covers ground not discussed in academic theology, writing at a popular level on issues such as marriage, parenting, finances, church leadership, etc.

Hiestand's assessment of these models expresses a genuine appreciation for them but also highlights their weaknesses. First, they both rely on the output of academic theologians. This has two problems: (1) academic theology does not scratch where the church itches; its approach to theological topics is not shaped by the church's needs. "We do not simply need to get more of existing theology into the church, but also to get more of the church into theology" (267) and neither the local nor the popular theologian will do this. (2) There is also a wide range of topics central to the church's mission which academic theology simply does not touch upon. We cannot draw down or popularise what isn't there. Our thinking on those issues is therefore relatively shallow.

Second, Hiestand expresses a concern that neither of these models encourage young theologians to think that pastoral ministry and theological research are compatible and so they are drawn towards the academy, reinforcing the divide.

With that in mind, and without wanting to deny the importance of these two models, Hiestand describes a third: the *ecclesial theologian*:

> The ecclesial theologian is, first and foremost, a theologian who writes robust, biblical, ecclesially centred theological reflection to other theologians. It includes, but pushes beyond the local theologian and popular theologian models, prosecuting a theological agenda consistent with the theological needs of the church. The ecclesial theologian counters the sentiment that says 'Deep, penetrating commentaries and books on the atonement – that stuff is for the academy. Pastors should stick to writing pop theology and Christian living stuff.' *Me genoito!* [by no means!] Expounding God's word and reflecting on the nature of the atonement etc.,
> (268) is the duty of bishops and elders and pastors.

Not, of course, that every pastor is gifted or called to be an ecclesial theologian. What Hiestand is arguing is simply that alongside local and popular theologians we need to glimpse the potential and recover the model of ecclesial theologians; "only by reuniting the office of pastor with the historical duty of the theologian [can we] begin to address the theological anemia of the church and the ecclesial anemia of theology" (271).

Reflections

At root this article is a plea for the church to recapture a desire for theological depth and then to meet that need. Hiestand wants the *supply* as well as the *demand* to come from the church. This raises a number of questions. First, there is the question of where the responsibility for theology actually lies. The division between the academy and the church means the church has outsourced the work of producing theology to the academy rather than seeing it as part of its calling.

In practice (and caricaturing things somewhat) some churches leave theology in the academy; they don't want to 'do theology' because it gets in the way of 'normal ministry.' Other churches will be grateful that theology is being produced but will still see that as *someone else's job*.

In all this I've been pondering Paul's words in 1 Tim 3:15 describing "God's household, which is the church of the living God, the pillar and foundation of the truth."

Where does responsibility for theology lie? Squarely with the church. It is the pillar and foundation of the truth.

That's not to say that the church can't then set up structures [conferences, training courses, theological colleges] beyond the local church in order to fulfil its calling, but it remains the church's calling. This means that although the article addresses PhD students and invites them to do their theology from within the church, really the responsibility to take the initiative lies with the church. So, there's something to reflect on about the role of the church.

Second, there is also an important thought here about the role of the pastor. Although Hiestand describes the "local theologian" as a possible model of ministry for a pastor it should surely be the way every pastor sees himself.

Wouldn't Paul hear Hiestand's description of "the theologically astute pastor who ably services the theological needs of a local church, most immediately through a preaching ministry" and think, "yes, that's what I mean by an elder."

Able to teach (1 Timothy 3:2), able to "encourage others by sound doctrine and refute those who oppose it" (Titus 1:9), equipping God's people for works of service (Ephesians 4:12). Of course, again, there are degrees of gifting and our background, training and circumstances will all shape what this looks like. But this is a pastor's calling: to be a local theologian, and, under God, to be the best local theologian he can be. Hiestand is right to say

"the theological, gospel integrity of the Christian community will never rise above the level of her pastors" (270).

For that reason, every pastor has an interest in the quality of theological resources he can get his hands on and, combining this with our first observation, he shouldn't simply think of himself as a consumer in this. He is a member of the church and the church is responsible for theology. The pastor has some responsibility for prospering the cause of theology within the church and seeing the church fulfil its charge to be the pillar and foundation.

Third, how serious is the situation? It is worth putting the article in some context. It belongs to a number of protests located in the United States against the professionalisation of ministry and the preference in seminaries for new books about business management over old books about theology. In the same vein David Wells sounds a lament in *The Courage to be Protestant*: "Gone is the older model of the scholar-saint, one who was as comfortable with books and learning as with the aches of the soul." On the other hand, there are more optimistic noises being made Stateside. For example, Owen Strachan's chapter at the start of *The Pastor as Scholar and the Scholar as Pastor* (Carson/Piper) is entitled "The Return of the Pastor-Scholar," citing the ministries and works of John Piper, Don Carson, Kevin Vanhoozer, Al Mohler, and Gerald Hiestand as generating new interest in the model.

David F. Wells, *The Courage to Be Protestant: Truth-Lovers, Marketers, and Emergents in the Postmodern World* (Grand Rapids: Eerdmans, 2008), 40. See also Al Mohler's article 'The Pastor as Theologian' at *www.albertmohler.com/2006/04/17/the-pastor-as-theologian-part-one*

Two closely related books have also recently been published from these circles: Gerald Hiestand and Todd Wilson, *The Pastor Theologian: Resurrecting an Ancient Vision* (Grand Rapids: Zondervan, 2015); Kevin J. Vanhoozer and Owen Strachan, *The Pastor as Public Theologian: Reclaiming a Lost Vision* (Grand Rapids: Baker, 2015).

On this side of the pond, things are certainly a little different. American management-speak probably had less impact than a brand of Australian plain-speaking pragmatism which galvanized a branch of conservative evangelicalism to get on with preaching the Bible and reaching the lost. Somewhat paradoxically the Australians invested heavily in theological training and scholarship and that investment wasn't entirely matched here, suggesting that perhaps we and not they were the pragmatists after all.

Alongside the pragmatism, there are a couple of other factors in play: amateurism (we still love a self-deprecating, self-taught eccentric) and a submissive reverence for 'the expert.' These mean that the pastor in the UK who wishes to fulfil his role as a local theologian faces two distinctly British challenges: that one isn't really supposed to be any good at anything except by accident or luck, and that there's no need to study so hard because we have the experts at the conferences or in the theological colleges and we can call them when things get sticky.

More positively, however, there are strands of Anglicanism and non-conformity that have always devoted themselves to theological study, expressed in fraternals, conferences and publications. There is also a proliferation of training courses and an increasing willingness to invest in the more intensive and residential formats. We also have a number of local, popular, and even the odd ecclesial theologian from many different church backgrounds who serve the church admirably, not least by their involvement in those training courses.

On the other hand there is still a sense that the church lacks the depth of thinking on several key issues of the day. It was striking to hear Glyn Harrison at the 2014 FIEC Leaders' Conference describe how much work there remains to do analysing the first and the twenty-first centuries' understandings of human sexuality. In conversations with pastors, one of the most frequently raised topics is that of cohabitation and yet there are hardly any works that address the issue with any rigour. These are not projects the secular academy is going to sponsor.

So, if Hiestand is at least partly right about the problem, what about his solution? Do we need 'ecclesial theologians'? Essentially the answer is "No, they don't exist" and "Yes we certainly do."

When I say they don't exist I mean that they are at the very least so rarely sighted that they are not going to be able to supply the resources that are needed. It is common for Athanasius, Luther, Calvin, Jonathan Edwards et al. to be cited as exemplars of a model we've lost but in truth they were (a) exceptional and (b) not full-time pastors when they were at their most productive. As even Hiestand notes, Luther was not a pastor in Wittenberg but "regularly participated in ecclesial disputes, pastoral training and was a frequent preacher" (268).

So there is a degree of romanticism about some of these wistful backward glances at historical pastor-theologians. On the other hand we do need to work out how churches can identify areas of theological need and plan to meet that need rather than wishing someone else would fix it.

In practice there are many more models of ministry than just the full-time ecclesial pastor-theologian. Some of our larger churches may well be able to support such a person but it is not the only avenue. Sabbaticals can be used for more than sermon series prep. Pastors or their assistants can be freed up to undertake some research part-time. Gospel partnerships, denominations and other groups can work together to resource projects or individuals.

And where then does *Primer* fit in? Centrally we want to equip pastors to be effective local theologians and to help them train up other leaders in their churches. With that in view, we plan in each issue to offer a digest of one area of theology, drawing on the treasures of ecclesial theology past and present and always steering towards its significance for the life and health of the church. We're convinced this is a conversation worth having. P